healthy eating for
diabetes

Antony Worrall Thompson with

Azmina Govindji BSc RD

healthy eating for
diabetes

Photography by Steve Lee

Kyle Books

contents

This edition published by Kyle Books in 2009, an imprint of Kyle Cathie Limited
www.kylecathie.com
Distributed by National Book Network
4501 Forbes Blvd., Suite 200, Lanham, MD20706
Phone: (301) 459 3366

First published in the U.S. in 2004 by Barnes & Noble Books

ISBN 978-1-904920-96-0

First published in Great Britain in 2003 by Kyle Cathie Ltd

Text © 2003 Antony Worrall Thompson and Azmina Govindji
Photography © 2003 Steve Lee
Book design © 2003 Kyle Cathie Limited

Senior Editor: Muna Reyal
Designer: Carl Hodson
Photographer: Steve Lee
Home economist: Jane Suthering
Assistant to home economist: Julian Biggs
Styling: Penny Markham
Copy editor: Anne Newman
Recipe analysis: Dr. Wendy Doyle
Production: Sha Huxtable

Library of Congress Control Number: 2008940721

Color reproduction by Sang Choy
Printed and bound in Singapore by Star Standard

important note
The information and advice contained in this book are intended as a general guide to healthy eating and are not specific to individuals or their particular circumstances. This book is not intended to replace treatment by a qualified medical professional. Neither the authors nor the publishers can be held responsible for claims arising from the inappropriate use of any dietary regime. Do not attempt self-diagnosis or self-treatment for serious or long-term conditions without consulting a medical professional or qualified doctor.

Dedication
To Frank Shiel, my new Dad and father-in-law, who was recently diagnosed with diabetes.

foreword by DRWF

Diabetes is an every day, every hour, and every minute type of problem.

Diabetes has no limits and no boundaries. It is a complex, life-changing disease that demands that you become intimately aware of all aspects of your health, particularly your diet. Good control, exercise, and healthy eating are the essential components to every diabetic's life.

I know this first hand, as my family has been affected by this tragic disease for more than 33 years. Throughout this time, I've come to understand that we each need to take charge of our health, and become our body's best advocate.

Healthy Eating for Diabetes is a wonderful new resource to help each of us seize and maintain control over diabetes and the constant threat of its complications.

The delicious recipes that Antony and Azmina demonstrate in this beautiful cookbook are healthy and fresh alternatives not only for diabetics, but also for all of the family and friends that love and care for them. I just know that this book will inspire and empower anyone who has been touched by diabetes to take the time to prepare healthy and fresh meals, each and every night. This cookbook is sure to become a welcome addition to my kitchen.

The Diabetes Research & Wellness Foundation® (DRWF) is a 501c3 organization for people who live with diabetes every day. Our motto is, "Staying healthy until a cure is found." We are working tirelessly to help find the cure for diabetes, and until that goal is achieved, we will help provide the care and self-management skills needed to combat the life-threatening complications of this terrible disease.

Over the past 15 years, DRWF has funded more than $30 million dollars towards research for the cure, and we will continue on until we have achieved our mission: Life without diabetes!

The Diabetes Research and Wellness Foundation provides essential resources for diabetics, including our monthly newsletter, *Diabetes Wellness News*, our diabetes helpline, and our free diabetes identification program.

Andrea G. Stancik
Executive Director of Diabetes Research & Wellness Foundation®

what is diabetes?

Have you been newly diagnosed with diabetes? Or does someone in the family have diabetes? If so, read on for the true facts on just what diabetes is, and how to live with it and still enjoy a full and active life.

When you have diabetes, the amount of glucose (sugar) in your blood is too high because your body is unable to use it properly. A hormone called insulin helps glucose to enter the cells where it is used as fuel by your body. If there is not enough insulin, or if the insulin you have is not working properly, then glucose can build up in your blood as a result.

Types of diabetes

✳ Type 1 or insulin-dependent diabetes occurs when there is a severe lack of insulin in the body. It is treated by insulin injections and a healthy range of foods.
✳ Type 2 or non-insulin-dependent diabetes is the most common type, and over 80 percent of people who have it are overweight. In type 2 diabetes, the body can still make some insulin, but not enough for its needs. It can be treated by a healthy diet alone, or by diet and tablets, or sometimes by diet and insulin injections.

What causes diabetes?

There is no one cause of diabetes and it seems to be caused by a combination of genetic and environmental factors. We know that it runs in families and we also know that if you are overweight, you are more likely to get type 2 diabetes.

There is no cure for diabetes yet, and there is no such thing as mild diabetes. The main aim of treatment is to avoid "highs" and "lows" in your blood glucose level. Together with a healthy lifestyle, this will help to improve your well-being and protect against long-term damage to your eyes, kidneys, nerves, and heart.

Knowing the tell-tale signs

One of the difficulties with diabetes is that you might actually be symptom-free (particularly if you have type 2). Many people are diagnosed only after a routine examination by their doctor. So, if you think you may have diabetes (for example, if you have a family history or one or more of the risk factors below), a simple blood test can put your mind at ease. Spotting the condition early will mean that it can be treated.

What to look out for
If you notice any of the following, it could be an indication that you have diabetes:

✳ increased thirst, especially for sweet drinks

✳ you go to the toilet a lot, especially at night

✳ you feel very tired

✳ you are losing weight unexpectedly

✳ itching of the genital organs or recurrent thrush

✳ blurred vision.

The above symptoms are characteristic of type 1 diabetes, which is easier to diagnose, and the symptoms can be quickly relieved with treatment. However, if you have type 2 diabetes, which is more common in people over forty, these symptoms may be less apparent or even nonexistent.

Low blood sugar

The medical term for low blood sugar is "hypoglycemia", although it is more commonly referred to as a "hypo." This is, generally speaking, most likely to occur in people treated with insulin. It can be caused by:

✳ missing a meal or snack

✳ engaging in strenuous activity without enough food beforehand

✳ injecting more insulin than is needed

✳ drinking alcohol on an empty stomach.

Sometimes, however, there may be no obvious reason for a hypo. Signs and symptoms of a hypo vary, but the common ones are light-headedness, a faint feeling, sweating, shaking, hunger, and confusion.

A hypo should be treated by immediately taking a dextrose tablet, sugared water, or a sugar lump to raise your blood sugar quickly, followed by (within half an hour) something more substantial (such as a glass of milk and a slice of toast) to maintain a good blood sugar level.

Syndrome X

You may have heard about the term Syndrome X and wondered what it was. It sounds like something from a science-fiction movie but it actually refers to a collection of medical conditions. These include:

✱ central obesity, which means a waist measurement of more than 37" for men (36" for South Asian men as they have been found to be even more at risk) and more than 32" in women

✱ poor blood sugar control

✱ high blood pressure

✱ abnormal blood fats including raised triglycerides and low HDL (the "good" form of cholesterol – see page 16)

✱ "sticky blood" with an increased tendency to form clots.

A diagnosis of Syndrome X is reached when three or more of these conditions occur together. Each of them is an independent risk factor for heart disease and having more than one condition increases the risk considerably.

What causes it?
Syndrome X is also sometimes referred to as "metabolic syndrome" or "insulin resistance syndrome." There appears to be a genetic factor at work, so having a family member with Syndrome X increases your risk. Current thinking is that all the conditions associated with it arise from one main cause: insulin resistance. Insulin resistance is a reduced sensitivity in the tissues of the body to the action of circulating insulin. As a result, the pancreas reacts by trying to produce more insulin, leading to high circulating levels in the blood. If the insulin resistance becomes severe, type 2 diabetes can develop.

How common is it?
Syndrome X seems to be very common in the Western world. Estimates from the USA and Scandinavia suggest that between 10 and 25 percent of adults show some degree of insulin resistance. Syndrome X is sometimes said to be "silent" since most people who have it are unaware of it.

Risk factors include obesity, a family history of type 2 diabetes, and a history of diabetes during pregnancy.

What can you do if you have Syndrome X?
Research has shown that both insulin resistance and the symptoms of Syndrome X can be improved by lifestyle changes, including physical activity and healthy eating. There is some research to suggest that a diet based mainly on foods with a low glycemic index (see page 12) may improve insulin sensitivity in people with type 2 diabetes, but their role in Syndrome X is not clear at present. The good news is that these approaches, if successfully adopted, are very effective in reducing the risk of heart disease and of developing type 2 diabetes.

Lifestyle Guidelines for Syndrome X

✱ Engage in physical exercise – activities such as brisk walking.

✱ Cut down on the amount of fat and especially saturated fat in your diet. Replace this with mono and polyunsaturated fats from vegetable sources and fish.

✱ Choose starchy carbohydrate and fiber-rich foods, fruit and vegetables.

✱ Keep your body weight to within 20 percent of ideal targets.

✱ Drink alcohol in moderation only.

✱ Don't smoke.

food facts

What you eat is the most important part of your diabetes treatment. Whether you need to take medication or not, the foods you choose and how often you eat, have a significant impact on your blood glucose. What you eat also affects the amount of fat (like cholesterol) in your blood. If you have diabetes, you already have an increased risk of developing heart disease, so watching what you eat is particularly important. Insulin or tablets are not a substitute for a healthy diet. There are lots of healthy eating tips in this book. It's a good idea to pick out the changes that you feel will easily fit into your lifestyle, choosing foods you enjoy. Don't think in terms of foods that you must or must not eat. Healthy eating is all about balance – selecting a variety of healthy foods you enjoy and not forcing yourself to eat foods you dislike.

A taste of the Mediterranean

The Mediterranean way of eating, with its abundance of olive oil, garlic, fish, nuts, fruit, and vegetables, has been associated with a lower risk of conditions such as coronary heart disease and cancer, so incorporating foods from Mediterranean cuisine into the diet for diabetes makes sense. And the good news is that recent research supports the idea that eating the right types of fat may be more important than making your fat intake really low. It has been shown that the total amount of fat eaten by people who live in Mediterranean countries is actually quite high, but when you take a closer look, you see that it's high in monounsaturated oils (such as olive oil), and omega-3 fats (such as those found in oily fish). Research suggests that even as little as an ounce a day of oily fish (such as salmon, herring, mackerel, and tuna) can significantly reduce the incidence of heart disease, and it even benefits those people who have already suffered a heart attack. People in Mediterranean countries also eat more fruit and vegetables, so they benefit from a good antioxidant intake (see page 22), as well as more garlic and the classic glass of red wine, both of which have been shown to have therapeutic properties. Garlic has been shown to thin the blood, helping it to flow more smoothly, while the active ingredients in red wine, phenols, act in a similar way to the antioxidant vitamins, so that one glass a day is thought to be protective against heart disease.

Starchy foods

Starchy carbohydrate foods (such as bread, rice, pasta, cereals, chapatis, and potatoes) are healthy and naturally low in fat. Many recipes is this book contain pasta, which is an excellent starchy food for people with diabetes. Starchy foods are also filling, and if they are cooked properly in minimal fat, they can be helpful if you are trying to lose weight. Whole-grain varieties of bread and cereals as well as the skin on potatoes are high in fiber. High-fiber starchy foods such as bran-based cereals and whole wheat bread are especially useful in preventing constipation. A high-fiber diet is good for the whole family, but remember that when you eat more fiber, it is important to drink more fluid. Try to drink at least six to eight cups of fluid each day.

Oat-based cereals, like porridge and muesli, are high in soluble fiber. These foods are often more slowly absorbed than starchy foods in general, and they can play a significant part in keeping your blood glucose within a healthy range. Instant hot oat cereals do contain soluble fiber, but because the oats have been "mashed up" they have less effect on slowing down the rise in blood glucose after meals.

It is important to spread your intake of starchy foods evenly through the day, and to eat regular meals. This helps to reduce fluctuations in your blood glucose levels.

Carbohydrates

Flicking through a newspaper, it is neither unusual nor surprising to see many articles on the latest trend in carbohydrates, whether they are telling you to "avoid wheat", that "starchy foods are fattening," or that "pasta is the best food ever invented." How are you to know what's best in the case of diabetes? And is all this conflicting advice, or do the experts agree? Let's review some of the more confusing issues here.

The chemical structure of carbohydrates affects how they are metabolized. Simple carbs are made up of shorter chains of sugar, while complex carbs are made up of longer structures.

Sugar ("simple" carbohydrates)	Starches ("complex" carbohydrates)
Glucose	Breads, including chapatis, pita
Fructose, found in fruit, some vegetables and honey	Tortillas, etc.
	Pasta, noodles
Sucrose, as in tabletop sugar	Rice
Maltose	Potatoes, plantains, cassava, yams
Lactose, found only in milk and milk products	Cereals

The low-carb way of eating

Low-carb diets, perhaps the best-known example of which is the Atkins diet, typically involve basing meals on meat, poultry, fish, eggs, and cheese, severely restricting all carbohydrate-rich foods such as bread, potatoes, pasta, rice, pizza, potato chips, cereals, and sugars. They also limit most fruits, some vegetables, and many alcoholic drinks.

Some of these diets allow large amounts of butter, oil, cheese, and fatty meats, but such diets tend to be high in protein. Too much protein can place a strain on the kidneys, and since people with diabetes may be at risk of developing kidney problems, a high intake may be harmful. While more carbohydrate is allowed when

you are trying to maintain the weight loss, the overall diet actually conflicts with the current international consensus for both good health and weight control. There really is not, at present, scientific evidence to support the need to go to such low-carb extremes, especially for someone with diabetes.

Are carbs acceptable?

So, is pasta in or out? Should you skip potatoes? Meals are best tailored to the individual, rather than everyone aiming for the same goals, since some people will do better on less starchy foods than others.

Most people with type 2 diabetes would benefit from losing weight, so filling up on starchy foods, which add calories, is unhelpful. If balanced meals and snacks are maintained, there's no reason why favorite starchy foods cannot be a part of the daily food intake. In fact, there are some carbohydrates that are actively encouraged – those with a low glycemic index (GI; see below).

When it comes to sugar, which is also a carbohydrate food, the advice is different, but again, forget the myth that you can't have any sweet tastes in diabetes – see page 15 for more on sugar.

Glycaemic index (GI)

When you eat carbohydrate foods (such as bread, potatoes, pasta, or cereals), the body digests the starch until, eventually, it becomes glucose (sugar). This can then be used by the body for energy and it is this glucose which contributes to the glucose levels in your blood.

Glucose also comes from other foods, but mainly from the starchy and sugary foods. So, is it as simple as just watching the starch and sugar in your diet? New research shows that not all carbohydrate foods have the same effect on blood glucose. Furthermore, the amount and type of fat, the type of fiber and even the way foods are cooked is more important.

The GI is a ranking of foods relating to how these foods affect blood glucose levels. The faster a food is broken down during digestion, the quicker the level of blood glucose will rise. Since one of the main aims of treatment of diabetes is to keep blood glucose levels steady throughout the day, foods which cause sharp rises are best kept to a minimum, except in special circumstances, such as illness, hypoglycemia (see page 8), or exercise. Foods that cause a rapid rise in blood glucose will have a high-GI, so the key is to choose more low-GI foods regularly (see pages 13 and 14). The effects from a low-GI meal can run into the following meal, which helps to keep blood glucose more even throughout the day.

Since low-GI foods reduce the peaks in blood glucose that often follow a meal, they may have a role in helping to prevent or reduce the risk of getting type 2 diabetes if you are at risk, as in Syndrome X (see page 9). Low-GI foods can help you to eat less as you feel fuller for longer. Research has also shown that people who follow an overall low-GI diet have a lower incidence of heart disease, and lower-GI diets have also been associated with improved levels of "good" cholesterol (see page 16).

Which foods should you go for?

"Whole" foods, such as whole-grains, and those high in soluble fiber, for example kidney beans, will take longer to be broken down by the body and will thus cause a slower rise in blood glucose. If you imagine how easy it is to digest puréed pea soup, which is already in small particles, it would make sense to suggest that the body doesn't need to mash this up for too long before it is ready to enter the bloodstream as glucose. Now imagine how much longer it would take to digest whole peas. The body needs to break down the skin of the peas before it even reaches the pulp, then it needs to break that down into a mush before it is small enough to enter the bloodstream. Whole peas will therefore make the blood glucose rise more slowly than the puréed soup. This is the case with most foods. Compare hummus to a whole chickpea casserole, mashed potatoes to a baked potato, and whole wheat bread to a seeded bread.

Look at the whole food

It's important to know that not all low- or medium-GI foods are recommended for good health. The addition of fat and protein, for example, slows down the absorption of carbohydrate, giving foods a lower GI, so that chocolate, for instance, has a medium GI because of its fat content. And potato chips and french fries actually have a lower GI than potatoes cooked without fat. Milk and other dairy products have a low GI because of their high protein content, and the fact that they contain fat. So, if you choose only low-GI foods, your diet could be unbalanced and high in fat,

which could lead to weight gain and an increased risk of heart disease. Overall balance is, then, the key to healthy eating, and the right mix of foods will not only ensure better control of your blood glucose, but will also help you to obtain the wide variety of nutrients needed for good health.

The table on page 15 gives a comparison of the GI levels of various foods. The GI of a food only tells you how quickly or slowly it raises the blood glucose when the food is eaten on its own, so you need to bear in mind that in practice, we generally eat foods in combination: bread is usually eaten with butter or margarine; potatoes are often eaten with meat and vegetables, etc. So cutting out all high-GI foods is not the answer; instead include more low-GI foods to lower the overall GI of meals.

Low-GI foods	Medium-GI foods	High-GI foods
Muesli and porridge	Beetroot	Bagels
Multi-grain and rye bread	Basmati rice	White & wholemeal bread
Fruit loaf	Potatoes, boiled	Water biscuits
Pasta	Rich tea biscuits	Glucose drinks
Baked beans	Pitta bread	Corn chips (tortilla crisps)
Lentils	Wheat biscuits (e.g.	Corn flakes
Apples, oranges and pears	(Weetabix)	Puffed wheat
Yogurt	Couscous	Puffed rice
Sweetcorn	Ice cream	Sugar-rich breakfast cereals
Bran cereals (e.g. All Bran,	Digestive biscuits	Sports drinks
Sultana Bran)	Honey	Waffles

The truth about sugar

Sugar is just calories; it has no benefits in terms of vitamins, minerals, protein, or any other nutrient. However, we cannot ignore the fact that sugary foods taste good! So, whether you have diabetes or not, the advice is simple: enjoy a range of foods, mainly fruit, vegetables, and starchy foods, and limit the amount of fatty and sugary foods you eat: you need not avoid them altogether.

In the past, it was believed that sugary foods automatically caused a rise in blood sugar and it therefore seemed to make sense to avoid these foods if you had diabetes. However, we now know that the effect of a particular food on blood sugar depends not only on how much sugar it contains, but also on a range of other factors including the way

in which it is cooked, how it is served (i.e., whole, mashed, or in between), and what is eaten with it.

A drink which is high in sugar, for example, when taken on an empty stomach or in between meals, will cause a quick rise in blood glucose because it is rapidly absorbed into the bloodstream. However, if it is taken mixed with food, especially at the end of a high-fiber meal, the rise will take place more slowly. This is especially true if your meal contains foods with a low glycemic index (see page 12). So, in short, small amounts of sugar are fine for people with diabetes if taken as part of an overall healthy eating plan, and ideally at the end of a meal.

Desserts
Having diabetes does not mean saying goodbye to desserts. All sorts of sweets

and puddings can be incorporated into your diet, particularly if you choose appropriate ingredients. Half-fat creams, low-fat instant dessert mixes, fresh and dried fruit, can all help to reduce the fat and sugar content of traditional desserts. To make your desserts even lower in fat, try using virtually fat-free fromage frais or low-fat plain yogurt. Base desserts on fruit as often as possible and try to eat two to three fruits a day.

Sweeteners

Artificial sweeteners made from aspartame, saccharin, and acesulfame potassium are sugar-free and will not cause a rise in your blood glucose levels. They may be used to sweeten foods but it is generally best to add them after cooking or in recipes that don't need to be heated since they sometimes develop a bitter aftertaste when heated to high temperatures.

They are not, however, a good substitute for sugar in baking. Again, it's all a matter of personal choice. If you prefer to use an artificial sweetener (which, incidentally, is also calorie-free), then you can choose to do so, for example, in cereals and desserts. This will give you a food which, in the end, is lower in sugar and calories than if you'd used sugar. However, if you prefer to use a little sugar, ensure that the other foods in your meal are healthy by including, for instance, high-fiber cereal (such as oatmeal) for breakfast, beans and legumes in your main meals, and fruit as the basis of desserts.

Fats

Advice given about fats can often sound confusing. If fats are so bad for you, how come some are essential? If soft spreadable fats are better than hard fats like butter, why the caution with "trans" fats in margarine? If a high blood cholesterol is unhealthy, how is it that foods which are high in cholesterol are not necessarily bad for you?

One of the key tips for eating well, whether you have diabetes or not, is to cut down on your fat intake. Saturated fat has been shown to raise a type of fat in your blood called cholesterol. A high blood cholesterol makes you more prone to heart problems. Since people with diabetes are at an increased risk of getting heart disease, watching your fat intake is particularly important.

The science behind cholesterol

Blood is delivered to the heart via the coronary arteries. As you get older, it is normal for these arteries to narrow, primarily as a result of Western lifestyle and food habits, which cause fatty deposits (atheroma) to be laid down within the artery walls. The fat then hardens (atherosclerosis), resulting in the reduction of the rate of blood flow. Also, it is likely that the hardened fat becomes damaged, and blood cells form a clot as a means of protection. A large clot can block the artery completely, causing a heart attack. If your blood cholesterol is high, you are more likely to develop atherosclerosis.

Fat is transported around the blood as lipids, which are carried in tiny particles called lipoproteins. Although having high blood cholesterol increases your chances of having a heart attack, some blood cholesterol is not harmful at all. Often termed "good" cholesterol, high-density lipoprotein (HDL) represents the cholesterol which is being taken away from the body tissues, back to the liver. Most of your cholesterol is, however, carried in the low-density lipoprotein (LDL) or "bad" cholesterol. A high LDL level can increase your risk of a heart attack since it leads to the formation of fatty deposits in the arteries.

Therefore, the higher your HDL, the lower your risk of heart disease.

Get your fats straight

Fats differ according to their chemical make-up. Saturated fats are associated with raised blood cholesterol, and so it makes sense to keep a watchful eye on

Did you know?

✳ Fat, weight for weight, provides twice the calories of starch or protein.

✳ Foods high in fat tend to be high in calories and are often also high in sugar.

✳ Essential fats are needed regularly in small amounts because they cannot be manufactured from other foods nor from within the body. Omega-3 and omega-6 fats – the essential fatty acids – are crucial for normal growth and development.

✳ Cutting down on fatty foods is the fastest way to reduce your calorie intake, but if you go too low you may get bored and drive yourself into an eating frenzy!

✳ Fat acts as an important carrier for fat-soluble vitamins (A, D, E, and K) in the bloodstream.

✳ Your liver produces cholesterol regardless of the cholesterol in your diet.

✳ Cholesterol in food has less effect on your blood cholesterol than animal (saturated) fats.

✳ The ratio of fats in your diet as well as the quality, has been shown to be beneficial to overall health (see above, "Get your fats straight").

them. You do need some, but experts such as the Department of Health's Food Standards Agency in the UK recommend that no more than 10 percent of your daily calorie intake should come from this group. The rest of your fat intake should come from monounsaturated and polyunsaturated fats.

Put simply:

∗ Saturated fats raise "good" and "bad" blood cholesterol (see page 16). They can also make the blood more "sticky," making it more likely to clot. So cut down on these fats.

∗ Polyunsaturated fats appear to lower both "good" and "bad" blood cholesterol. Omega-3 and omega-6 fats are essential fatty acids that belong to this group. Omega-3s are the ones we should make a more conscious effort to eat more of, since we already get plenty of omega-6s from margarines and spreads.

∗ Monounsaturated fats lower "bad" cholesterol and are thought to raise "good" blood cholesterol. They are, therefore, recommended in preference to polyunsaturated fats. Hence, these are your best friends.

∗ Trans fats are usually by-products of hydrogenation, a process used to make unsaturated fats firm and spreadable. Research has shown that, like saturates, they raise blood cholesterol. Trans fats are found in processed foods like cookies, cakes and pastries (check the packages).

Fats	Sources	Recommendations
Monounsaturates	Olive oil, canola (rapeseed oil), peanut oil, spreads made from these oils	Replace saturated fats with these wherever possible
Omega-3 polyunsaturated fats	Fish oils, canola (rapeseed oil), olive oil, spreads made from fish oils, linseeds, soy beans	Eat more. Choose one portion of oily fish a week
Omega-6 polyunsaturated fats	Soy margarines, sunflower spreads, and sunflower, soy bean, safflower, corn, and grapeseed oils	Replace saturates with these, but eat in moderation
Trans fats	Hydrogenated spreads, processed foods made with trans fats	Keep to a minimum, remove from diet where possible
Saturates	Butter, lard, animal suet, processed foods made with saturates, fatty meat, skin on poultry	Cut down
Cholesterol	Eggs, shellfish, variety meats	Eat in sensible amounts as part of an overall low-fat diet

∗ Dietary cholesterol has little effect on blood cholesterol (see "Did you know," page 16). A low-fat diet will generally also be low in cholesterol, so you need not be overly conscious of cholesterol levels in food (unless you have a blood disorder, which specifically requires dietary cholesterol modification).

Reducing fats
Use cooking-oil sprays, which are often a mixture of oil and water (make your own using one part oil to seven parts water, or use a drizzle of olive or canola oil), or a small amount of butter in cooking. Try reduced-fat dairy products, such as low-fat or skim milk, half-fat cheese, and low-fat yogurt. Base salad dressings on low-fat plain yogurt and lemon juice, or buy fat-free dressings.

Protein

The majority of people in the Western world eat more than enough protein, and deficiency is extremely rare. Some surveys suggest that in the UK, we get at least 50 percent more protein than we need because of our ever-increasing portion sizes, especially of meat and dairy products. Too much protein can place a strain on and damage the kidneys, as they struggle to get rid of the excess.

People with diabetes may be at higher risk of developing kidney problems (nephropathy) and are therefore advised to keep proteins to sensible amounts and avoid higher-than-average intakes. This is especially important if you also have high blood pressure, which could increase the potential for damage.

If you already have kidney damage, you may be advised to limit protein intake more strictly, and the specialist advice of a registered dietitian will be necessary

Which protein foods are best?
There are vegetable (e.g., beans, legumes, nuts) and animal (e.g., meat, dairy products) sources of protein. Other than in the case of lean meat, fish, and low-fat dairy products, animal sources do tend to be higher in saturated fat. Studies have found lower blood cholesterol and blood pressure, and better blood-sugar control in people with diabetes who follow predominantly plant protein-based diets rather than in those who follow animal-based ones.

This doesn't mean you must become a vegetarian. Simply vary your meals so that you include a good range of vegetarian foods often.

All proteins are made up from building blocks called amino acids, some of which are essential to the body. Vegetable proteins tend to be lacking in one or more essential amino acids but if you mix them together, you can achieve the right balance. Many vegetarian dishes are based on this principle. The table (left) offers tips on how to combine vegetable protein foods to get the best mix.

Combined food group	Foods	Example dish
Cereals and legumes	Wheat and navy beans	Bruschetta with white bean purée and raw mushrooms (page 78)
	Rice and kidney beans	Jamaican rice and peas Vegetable chile
	Rice or noodles and soybeans	Tofu stir-fry
	Wheat and lentils	Lentil soup and bread
	Rice and lentils	Dhal curry and rice
	Corn and beans	Tortilla and refried beans
Cereals and nuts	Wheat and peanuts	Peanut butter sandwich
	Wheat and nuts	Nut roast with bread crumbs Belgian endive salad with walnuts and croutons (page 65
Legumes and seeds	Chickpeas and	Hummus sesame seed paste

Fruit and vegetables

These foods contain important vitamins that are needed for health, whether you have diabetes or not. A diet that contains plenty of fruit and vegetables will provide more fiber, especially the soluble variety, and more antioxidant vitamins, and will usually be lower in fat. The antioxidant vitamins, beta-carotene (which is converted to vitamin A in the body), vitamins E and C, have been linked to a lower incidence of heart disease, some cancers, and gut problems.

It is recommended that you eat at least five portions daily. Try to choose fruit and vegetables of varying colors, cook them quickly, and serve them as whole as possible rather than puréed.

How much is enough?
For good health, you should aim for 14 ounces, or about five three-ounce portions per day. Potatoes are classified as starchy carbohydrates, so they don't count.

What constitutes a portion?
✻ Medium apple, pear, orange, banana

✻ Large slice of melon or pineapple

✻ Cupful of strawberries or grapes

✻ ½–1 tablespoon of dried fruit

✻ 1 small glass of fresh fruit juice

✻ 2 tablespoons of cooked vegetables

✻ Small serving of salad vegetables, e.g., a carrot, a tomato, or a small bowl of mixed greens

✻ 2 tablespoons of canned vegetables, e.g. corn, green beans

What about juice and dried fruit?
As you can see from the list, dried fruit and fresh fruit juice do count. However, it is best to choose juice as only one of your five portions, since the valuable fiber has been removed.

From the diabetes point of view, drinking large amounts of fruit juice, even if this is unsweetened, may make your blood glucose rise sharply. This is because the natural sugar in a liquid form is rapidly absorbed by the body. If you like fresh fruit juice, take it with a meal rather than on its own. Alternatively, choose a diet drink.

Legumes, such as beans and lentils, are good because they are high in soluble fiber, which helps to control blood glucose levels (see page 13), but they can only be counted as one portion a day. This is because they don't contain the range of nutrients you get from other sources, such as green leafy vegetables, carrots, and tomatoes.

Antioxidants

These much-praised substances are found naturally in fruit and vegetables. They include vital vitamins such as vitamin A, C, and E, as well as lycopene (concentrated in tomatoes), flavanoids (found in tea), and selenium.

Antioxidants are thought to be protective since they "mop up" free radicals, which are present in the body but can cause some of the problems associated with heart disease and cancer. Free radicals are by-products of normal body processes but cigarette smoke, ultraviolet light, illness, and pollution increase their production.

And lycopene, which is concentrated in tomatoes, becomes more potent when the tomatoes are processed. So smothering pasta with a jar of tomato-based pasta sauce might be cheating from the culinary point of view, but will ensure that your meal is packed with hidden benefits.

Do supplements do the trick?

The brightly colored red, yellow and orange vegetables are particularly rich in antioxidants, especially beta-carotene. Packed with cancer-fighting power, these phyto-chemicals are present in fresh fruit and vegetables in precisely the quantities and combination Mother Nature intended. So taking a supplement with one or two of them just won't do the same job as the real foods themselves.

Meat, fish, nuts, pulses and eggs

These foods are rich in protein and many are good sources of vitamins and minerals, such as iron and zinc. However, meat can be high in saturated fat, so it is best to choose lean cuts and to minimize the oil you use in cooking. See "Reducing fats" on page 17 for advice on lower-fat choices.

Meat dishes can be made healthier by adding beans or vegetables. This adds fiber, makes the meal go further, and generally provides fewer calories per plate.

Salt and hypertension

High blood pressure makes you more prone to heart conditions. Since eating too much salt is linked with high blood pressure, cutting down may be protective. Salt is the common name for sodium chloride and it is the sodium part of salt which is harmful if taken in excess. It's estimated that the average adult in the US consumes more than double the sodium their body needs. Most of the salt comes from manufactured foods, and it is very likely that you are taking in far more than this amount each day, especially if you rely heavily on processed meals and snacks. For good health, it is recommended that you keep your total daily salt intake (including that in manufactured foods) to six grams, or just over one teaspoon. This is equivalent to 2.5g of sodium.

Salt sense

✳ Measure the amount of salt you add in cooking and gradually cut down till a recipe that serves four people contains around a half teaspoon of salt.

✳ Avoid adding salt at the table.

✳ Experiment with herbs and spices, using, for example, freshly ground spices, dried and fresh herbs, paprika, and freshly milled black pepper. If you find it hard to get used to a less salty flavor, you can try a salt substitute. Low-salt products (such as vegetables canned in water, unsalted butter) can be used as replacements.

✳ For varied flavors, try lime juice, balsamic vinegar, and chile sauce.

✳ Read food labels carefully. Salt may appear as sodium, sodium chloride, monosodium glutamate, or bicarbonate of soda. Multiply the sodium figure by 2.5 to find the salt content.

✳ Cut down on salty foods such as salted potato chips, nuts, crackers, and pastries.

✳ Salted and smoked foods such as bacon, sausages, smoked fish, some canned fish, and other processed foods are often loaded with salt. Whenever possible, use fresh foods such as fish, lean meat, fruit, and fresh vegetables. They have only a small amount of salt.

Salt substitutes

If you need to cut down on salt, you will find that in time your taste buds adjust and you will begin to prefer the taste of less salty foods. If you are still craving a salty flavor, however, a salt substitute is a practical and convenient way of reducing your salt intake. Read the label – some leading brands offer up to two thirds less sodium than ordinary salt, and you can use them in cooking and at the table. They are not recommended for people with kidney problems, however, as they contain potassium which can have a harmful effect on diseased kidneys.

Alcohol

If you have diabetes, there's no reason why you shouldn't enjoy a drink, unless, of course, you have been advised to avoid alcohol for another medical reason. Observe the safe drinking limit for everyone: between 21 and 28 units a week for men (or 3–4 units a day) and between 14 and 21 units a week for women (or 2-3 units a day). Note that these are the maximum recommended amounts, and drinking less is preferable. Try to space your drinking throughout the week and to have two or three alcohol-free days each week.

Safe drinking

Alcohol can cause hypoglycemia (a "hypo," or low blood glucose, see page 8) if you are taking insulin or certain tablets for your diabetes, and the higher the alcohol content (such as in hard liquor), the more likely it is to cause a hypo. These guidelines may help to prevent this:

✳ Avoid drinking on an empty stomach. Always have something to eat with a drink, and especially afterwards if you have been out drinking. This is because the hypoglycemic effect of alcohol can last for several hours.

✳ Choose low-alcohol drinks; avoid special diabetic beers, as these are higher in alcohol.

✳ If you enjoy hard liquor, try to use the sugar-free/slimline mixers.

✳ If you count the amount of carbohydrate you eat, don't include the carbs from alcoholic drinks.

✳ Drink less if you are trying to lose weight, and consume no more than seven units of alcohol per week.

---

1 unit of alcohol is equal to:

✳ One 10-ounce glass of beer

✳ One small (2 fl. oz.) glass of sherry, aperitif, or liqueur

✳ 1 small 4-ounce glass of wine

✳ One ounce of hard liquor

latest developments

In spite of the fact that all sorts of new information are emerging about diabetes, you may find that your treatment still remains the same if the new dietary advice is not appropriate for you. In this section we look at the most up-to-date developments in dietary information about diabetes, so that you can be even better informed.

The Dose Adjustment For Normal Eating programme (D.A.F.N.E.)

D.A.F.N.E. is an educational program for people with insulin-treated diabetes. It was developed in Germany in 1987 and it has been very successful in helping people with diabetes to manage their condition better. Several trials are currently under way in the UK to see if the benefits can be repeated here, but it is not available nationally.

On the program, people with diabetes attend an intensive five-day course as part of a small group. They are encouraged to choose freely what they wish to eat and then taught to estimate the carbohydrate content for the quantity and type of foods and drinks chosen. They then adjust their insulin dose on a meal-by-meal basis as appropriate. In effect, they are learning how to adapt their insulin to their lifestyle, not their lifestyle to their insulin.

Initial reports from both the UK and Germany have found that for adults with moderate to poor diabetes control, training in D.A.F.N.E. seems to improve blood glucose levels compared with standard care. The studies have also found a reduction in frequency of hypo-glycemia, with effects lasting over several years of treatment.

Prior to the introduction of D.A.F.N.E., the dietary restrictions imposed on people with type 1 diabetes affected their overall quality of life. People using D.A.F.N.E. now say that they enjoy more flexibility and the freedom to eat what and when they like. Furthermore, it has been noted that self-esteem improves. In D.A.F.N.E., participants learn from each other as well as from the facilitators, and for many, it is the first chance they have had to take time out to concentrate on managing their own diabetes.

Are there any problems associated with D.A.F.N.E.?
Some people have some difficulty in dealing with the complexities of the carbohydrate-counting and in grasping the principles involved. In some cases, it is also necessary to increase the number of insulin injections. Two background doses of medium-/long-acting insulin are needed at the start and end of the day, along with another injection for each meal or snack. In addition, very intense blood glucose monitoring is encouraged which can be inconvenient at times.

The course does call for considerable commitment on the part not only of the participant but also of the facilitators. Time away from work, school, or home may be required in order to participate.

Is D.A.F.N.E. also used for type 2 diabetes?
D.A.F.N.E. has also been tested for people with insulin-treated type 2 diabetes in Germany but the results have not yet been fully evaluated. The types of diabetes are very different in many ways and there are factors such as insulin resistance (see page 9) and the effects of physical activity which make treatment more complex.

Folic acid and the heart

Folic acid (sometimes referred to as folate) is a water-soluble B vitamin. Interest in it has grown since it was found to help prevent neural tube defects like spina bifida in babies. This is why women who are seeking to become pregnant and those in their first twelve weeks of pregnancy are advised to take a 400mcg supplement of folic acid each day.

However, did you know that it may also be helpful in reducing heart disease risk, which is a common complication of diabetes? Folic acid acts to lower the levels of a substance known as homocysteine in the blood. High levels of homocysteine are a risk factor for development of heart disease, stroke, and peripheral vein disease.

Sources of folic acid
Folic acid occurs naturally in many foods including fruit (especially oranges and orange juice), vegetables (dark leafy vegetables such as broccoli, brussels sprouts, and spinach), potatoes, beans, legumes, whole grains, milk and yogurt. It is also added to many refined cereal-based foods (indeed all cereal foods in the USA are now routinely fortified with it) and soft-grain bread (check the labels) – yet another good reason for people with diabetes to eat more of these foods.

Chromium and diabetes

Chromium is a trace mineral needed by the body in very small amounts. It helps in the maintenance of normal blood sugar levels, mainly by enhancing the action of insulin. It also seems to play a part in maintaining healthy cholesterol levels and in weight control.

People with a deficiency of chromium can develop impaired glucose tolerance (see page 9), which is improved by chromium supplementation. However, chromium is found naturally in a wide range of foods and most people with type 2 diabetes do not seem to be chromium-deficient, nor do they appear to be any more at risk of developing a deficiency. Nevertheless, this has led researchers to question whether supplements may be of benefit to people with diabetes.

Studies have been carried out using large doses of chromium at a level far above that which could be obtained by diet alone. Few of the studies are well designed and controlled, and the results are somewhat mixed. Some studies, notably in people with type 2 diabetes living in China, found that very high doses of chromium led to an improved blood sugar control. However, it is not clear if these findings would be applicable in other countries. Many other studies have either been inconclusive or have shown no benefit. Research in the UK looked at moderate doses of chromium, such as could be obtained from diet, but found no benefit to glucose tolerance or blood fat levels in adults with type 2 diabetes. Clearly more research is needed in order for the role of chromium to become clear. At present, most diabetes organizations around the world do not recommend supplements.

Current guidelines from Diabetes UK are that chromium should only be given as a supplement where a clear deficiency has been diagnosed. Otherwise people with type 2 diabetes should try to follow a healthy and varied diet including known sources of chromium (see the table below) in order to rule out the possibility of deficiency.

Animal sources	Vegetable sources
Lean meat	Whole grains
Variety meats, especially liver	Brewers' yeast
Oysters	Nuts and seeds Vegetables and legumes

recipe tips for diabetes

All the recipes in this book are in line with healthy eating principles and they generally use low-fat, low-glycemic index ingredients as appropriate. At times, you will find that some dishes may appear to be "no-go areas" for people with diabetes, but we want to dispel the myth that people with diabetes need a special diet.

All your favorite foods can be incorporated into a healthy way of eating – it's getting the combinations right that's important, and making sure that you choose a variety. Tempting desserts and main meals cooked in creamy sauces may sound off limits, but these recipes have been originated with diabetes in mind, using ingredients such as lean meat, fromage frais, half-fat crème fraîche, lower-fat Greek yogurt, and skim milk. Asian-style dishes are served with steamed rice rather than fried rice, and in some recipes, fat has been trimmed off meat after cooking, such as in Ham Bollito (page 120), so that the fat content will actually be lower than in the analysis given in the recipe.

Cooking tips

✳ Select lean cuts of meat and trim off visible fat. Try to cook meat without adding fat by broiling, roasting, and braising. Avoid using the juices from roast meat for gravy.

✳ Remove the skin from poultry and remember that the thigh and leg pieces are highest in fat.

✳ Grill or broil chops, sausages, and burgers, and let the fat drain off.

✳ If you need to fry foods, try a cooking-oil spray on a non-stick pan.

✳ Use complex carbohydrate foods such as bread, cereals, pasta, and potatoes. Just watch the amount of fat you put on them: choose lower-fat spreads and dairy products.

✳ Remember the Mediterranean "musts" (see page 10) – garlic, fruit, vegetables, fish, nuts, beans, lentils.

✳ Select foods with a low glycemic index, (GI; see page 12). Foods that are high in soluble fiber, such as rye, whole-grain, and soft-grain white bread, peas, corn, beans, lentils, citrus fruits, and rolled oats, all have a low GI. Dried legumes such as beans, corn, peas, and lentils are generally low in fat and calories, and help to fill you up.

✳ Include lots of fish and try to include oily fish such as salmon, herring, and mackerel once a week. Choose drained, canned tuna in brine rather than in oil – the former has half the fat!

✳ Nuts, although high in fat, can be part of a healthy lifestyle. Research shows that a handful of peanuts or almonds can help to lower your risks of heart disease. Nuts are best used as an ingredient in a main meal rather than as a snack, especially if you are overweight.

Skip these...	... and try these instead!
Butter on bread	Bread dipped in a little olive oil and balsamic vinegar
Cheddar cheese	French Brie or low-fat cream cheese
Rich desserts	Fruity desserts
French fries or mashed potato	Whole potatoes boiled in their skins
Fatty meat	Lean meat, poultry without the skin, fish
Flaky pastry	Phyllo pastry with skim milk between layers
Mayonnaise	Reduced-calorie mayonnaise or fat-free dressings
Full-fat dairy products, e.g., full-fat milk/cheese, butter	Reduced-fat foods, e.g. lowfat milk, half-fat cheese, reduced- or low-fat spreads
Cooking oil for frying	Spray oil for greasing and shallow-frying, a little olive oil or canola (rapeseed) oil for stir-frying, sautéeing, etc.
Potato chips and salty snacks	Home-made popcorn, Melba toasts, pretzels, bread sticks
Rich cakes	Scones, fruit loaf, sponge cake

eating out

In today's hectic lifestyle, food on the go is becoming more and more common, and keeping an eye on the fats and figures can often become quite difficult as a result. What's more, fast food isn't necessarily healthy food, and often convenience overtakes health. So what are the best choices you can make to fit in with the chaos of modern-day life?

Going for an Indian

Opt for chicken, shrimp, or vegetable dishes rather than lamb or beef, which tend to be higher in fat – tandoori chicken, with plain boiled rice and some cucumber raita is a good choice. Tikka dishes or a small portion of grilled kabobs make good appetizers. Opt for dhal (lentil) dishes instead of veggie curries. They tend to be less oily. Pilau rice is fried rice, often with colored grains – order boiled rice to keep the calories low. Basmati rice also has a low GI (see page 12), which is good news.Ask if your poppadam can be microwaved or grilled, and your chapatis or naan served dry.

Some restaurants refer to Indian cheese, paneer, as cottage cheese, but watch out as it's actually full-fat cheese.

Steak fries and french fries

Thick-cut fries absorb less fat than thin-cut ones, since the thin ones have a larger surface area, but do watch out for those massive portion sizes that now appear standard. If you're really hungry, you're better off sharing a small portion of fries and making them into a french fry sandwich (no butter, of course). This will help to fill you up and reduce the amount of oil you have.

Try also bringing your fries home and placing them on paper towels – if you want to microwave them, do so for a few seconds on the paper towels and see the fat soak in. If you've bought batter-coated, deep-fried fish, you could take the batter off the fish, or if you want to be neat, place the fish, skin side down, on a plate. Use your fork, and eat the top layer of batter with the fish only, leaving the skin side on the plate.

For a healthier option, go for broiled fish, if available, ketchup, bread roll, and a salad accompaniment.

Burger binge

The fat content of the classic mega-size burgers is variable, since often they are fried. Top this with a dressing and cheese and the calories start to soar. A burger can still be acceptable on occasions, however, unless you pile on the fries and soft drink, in which case things do start to get a little out of hand. And the veggie-burger option is not necessarily any more virtuous. This is generally still cooked in fat and served with a creamy dressing. Choose thick-cut fries where possible and ask for a regular-sized portion rather than a large one, which will save you half the calories.

Order diet drinks (around 10 teaspoons less sugar than regular) and ask for "no dressing" and/or "no cheese" and you could make a difference to the fat content. Ketchup is preferable to the creamy sauces.

Finally, munch through an apple or banana before going to the burger bar, otherwise you might be tempted to go for a large!

Going Greek

Order grilled fish, grilled lean lamb, or a kabob. Traditional Greek staples, such as moussaka, taramasalata, and hummus are high in fat and loaded with calories. Fill up on tzatziki – a low-fat mixture of yogurt, cucumber, and garlic – with a small piece of pita bread, instead. Undressed Greek salad without the feta cheese can also be very satisfying. Drizzle on some fresh lime juice and smother in coarsely ground black pepper.

A veggie option like falafel is usually deep-fried and therefore not necessarily lower in calories. Have fewer falafel balls and fill the pita bread with some tzatziki and loads of salad.

Chinese food

A common pitfall when eating Chinese, Indian, and Thai meals is ordering group dishes. Try to give yourself a full plate at the beginning of a meal and stop when it's finished. Pile up the salad and vegetables as they help to fill you up.

Order plain boiled rice or noodles rather than the special fried varieties. Soft noodles with vegetables (such as a chow mein dish) are preferable to crispy ones. Go for steamed dishes, like a whole steamed fish with ginger, steamed vegetables, and steamed rice. Choose healthy appetizers like satay dishes with chile dipping sauce, and finish with fresh fruit or a scoop of ice cream rather than the fried fritters.

Pasta and pizza

Remember that pasta has a low GI (see page 12), so order it often. Ask for a fresh tomato sauce, which tends to be lower in fat than cream-based sauces, and say "no" to the Parmesan cheese. Even the smallest, thinnest restaurant pizzas have around 500 Calories, so go for a thin-base pizza with masses of vegetable toppings. Steer clear of extra cheese, pepperoni, and deep-pan bases.

Veggie eating

It's often thought that vegetarian foods are healthier, but this is not always the case. Dishes that are based on eggs and cheese can be high in fat – Cheddar cheese, for example, has around 30 percent fat, mostly saturated. And don't be fooled into thinking that all foods bought from a healthfood store are good for you. Many can be high in fat and sugar, and even though they may have been made with whole wheat flour, they are not necessarily healthy.

If you are vegetarian, legume vegetables such as beans and lentils provide a valuable source of protein and have a low GI (see page 12). Use these together with starchy foods like rice and pasta to prepare perfectly balanced meals (see the table on page 18).

shopping

As we have seen so far, diabetes is about sensible and varied eating habits – not specialist healthfood shopping. Imagine your shopping cart is divided into thirds. One third should be made up of fruit and vegetables; another should consist of bread, other cereals, and potatoes. The rest of the cart should contain equal amounts of meat and fish, milk and dairy food, and even less fatty or sugary food. So try to spend more time looking at the variety of fruit and vegetables and starchy cereals available, and less time on fatty snack foods. This will help you to make healthy choices and will also add variety to your diet. Some people find that shopping on the Internet stops them from buying foods from less healthy aisles, as they are not tempted by the smells of the bakery.

What about convenience foods?

We are all tempted, at one time or another, by the myriad convenience foods on display, be they ready-meals, pasta sauces, or desserts. Can they really be part of a healthy diet? Is it possible to mix and match to make them healthy?

Once again, it's all about balance and moderation. Many will be lower in starchy carbohydrate and fiber than homemade versions. If you find that this is the case, you can complement them with some extra grainy bread or a baked potato. Another good tip is to get into the habit of serving them with extra vegetables or salad.

You may be concerned that quick or convenient foods may be high in fat, sugar, and salt, all of which are relatively cheap ways for manufacturers to add flavor. But how can you tell? Sometimes it's easiest to look out for the "healthy eating" logo used by all the major supermarkets, but you should take extra care with labels boasting "healthy" on desserts and cakes, as they might be lower in fat but also higher in sugar, which does not necessarily mean that they are lower in calories.

Food labelling

Many foods make nutritional claims on their labels but research shows that consumers are very dubious as to how useful they really are. By law, there are specific requirements a product must meet in order make a nutritional or nutrient claim, and these are shown in the table below. Such claims may indicate a healthier choice, but bear in mind that this is all relative, since a reduced-fat version of a high-fat food could still be a high source of fat.

In the past, manufacturers have sometimes added to the confusion by using "percent fat-free" claims, but an "85 percent fat-free" food will still contain a hefty 15 percent fat! Nowadays this misleading practice has been controlled, with the exception of the reasonable "97 percent fat-free" claim on some products which contain only three percent fat.

Guidelines to common nutrient claims (Food Standards Agency 2002)

Nutritional claim	Definition (per 100g or 100ml)	Example
Low sugar Low fat Low sodium	Contains less than 5g sugar Contains less than 3g fat Contains less than 40mg sodium	Sugar-free custard Low-fat rice pudding Low-salt foods
Reduced sugar Reduced fat Reduced salt	Contains 25 percent less sugar, fat, or salt than standard product	Reduced-sugar jams Reduced-fat spreads Reduced-salt baked beans
Sugar free	Contains less than 0.2g sugar	Sugar-free jellies Sugar-free sodas (may be called "diet")
No added sugar/ unsweetened	Contains no sugars or no added foods that are composed mainly of sugars	Unsweetened fruit juices

Understanding nutritional information on food labels

While the ingredients list will tell you what's in a food, it does not tell you how much. Ingredients are listed in descending order of weight, so the first ingredient will be present in the largest quantity and the last ingredient will be the smallest. This can be useful up to a point but the actual nutritional content is far more relevant. Even if sugar is near the top of the list, it does not necessarily mean that the food in question is packed with sugar. (Also remember that sugar does come in different guises, such as sucrose, dextrose, glucose syrup, maltose, etc.; see the table on page 12.)

The Guideline Daily Amounts (GDAs) listed on food labels provide information on the average recommended nutrient content in a healthy diet for an adult of normal body weight. Exact needs will vary between individuals according to age, weight, and physical activity level. Nevertheless GDAs can help you to see how and whether a particular food might fit into your diet.

How do you compare foods?

Nutritional information can be used to tell you whether a food has a little or a lot of the listed nutrients. The table below provides guidelines to help you to determine this.

When looking at food labels, it is good practice to consider how often and in what amounts you would normally eat the food. A food may be high in fat and/or sugar, but if you eat only small amounts of it occasionally, that's acceptable.

For such foods, you should refer to the "per 100g" value; this is also useful for comparing two similar products such as ready-made sauces, to see which is healthier. In the case of foods that you eat more frequently or in larger amounts, it is more appropriate to use the "per serving" value.

Guideline Daily Amounts of nutrients for adults

Nutrient	Men	Women
Fat	95g	70g
Saturated fat	30g	20g
Sugar	70g	50g
Salt	7g	5g
Fiber	20g	16g

How to judge how much of a particular ingredient a food contains

A lot	A little
20g fat	3g fat
5g saturates	1g saturates
10g sugars	2g sugars
0.5g sodium	0.1g sodium
1.5g salt	0.3g salt
3g fiber	0.5g fiber

Healthy shopping tips

✳ Watch out for ever-increasing portion sizes on ready meals and snacks such as sandwiches, chips, and chocolate bars. Just switching from a standard bag of potato chips to a large bag would cause up to 13 1/2 pounds in weight gain over a year without changing anything else!

✳ Canned foods such as fruit, vegetables, legumes and fish can be useful. Look for those labeled "reduced" or "no added" sugar or salt.

✳ Don't forget dried and frozen foods too – often just as nutritious and more convenient.

✳ Try to avoid shopping when you're hungry. Shop after a meal, make a shopping list, and stick to it.

✳ Avoid foods such as cookies and chocolates labeled "suitable for diabetics." They are usually expensive and have limited nutritional benefit. Since these are unlikely to form a major part of what you eat, you'd be better off just having a small amount of a standard product.

✳ Many supermarkets provide leaflets for people with diabetes, guiding them to healthy choices. Some even organize "store tours" run by local registered dietitians. Consumers find these informative, enjoyable, and a great way to view their regular store in a different light. Why not approach the customer services desk at your local store about this, to generate demand?

weight management

Perhaps surprisingly, a heavy person burns more calories than a light person does, which destroys the myth that overweight people burn fewer calories when they exercise – often people who are overweight will blame their situation on a slow metabolism. It is possible to boost your metabolism by combining aerobic exercise and strength exercises.

Calories

The term "calorie" is loosely used to describe the energy value of a food when the body burns it up. However, when talking about the measurement of energy, and hence how many calories a food has, the term kilocalories (or kcals) is used on British food labels, while "Calories" is used on North American food labels. On North American labels, you will notice that the calorific value is given "per serving", and the size of a "serving" varies, depending on what the product is.

All the foods you eat provide calories, but some, generally those that are high in fat, are more concentrated in calories. For example, an apple, which is low in fat and high in fiber, will contain around 50 Calories, whereas an equivalent weight of Cheddar cheese will provide around eight times as many. Each gram of pure fat provides nine Calories, whereas a gram of protein or a gram of carbohydrate will provide around four Calories. This is why frying a food can have a significant effect on the total Calorie value.

Are you in shape?

Your ideal weight range depends on your height, and dietitians and doctors use each individual's body mass index (B.M.I.) to calculate this. To find your B.M.I., take your weight (in kilograms), and divide it by your height (in metres squared):

$$B.M.I. = \frac{weight\ (kg)}{height\ (m)^2}$$

The most desirable range is a B.M.I. of between 20 and 24. A larger B.M.I. is taken as an indication of being overweight, and the higher that figure is, the more overweight you are.

The 'fruit salad' theory

Are you an "apple," that is, someone whose waist is bigger than their hips, or a "pear," someone whose hips are bigger than their waist?

This may sound unimportant, but in fact, real scientific theories have been formulated using this information. Central obesity, or putting weight on around the abdomen, is said to be associated with resistance to insulin, which in turn has been shown to be a risk factor in coronary heart disease (see Syndrome X, page 9). People with a higher waist measurement have a raised risk of diabetes and heart disease. A waist measurement of more than 37 inches for men and more than 32 inches in women is considered to carry a risk. Men of South Asian origin have been found to be even more at risk, so ideal waist measurements in their case need to be less than 36 inches.

It would, therefore, appear that being more pear-shaped may actually offer some protection. Eating well and taking regular physical activity can help to reduce excess abdominal fat.

Steps to success

Before you begin your new healthy lifestyle, make a list of all the positive benefits you feel it will give you. Your list may include things like helping you to fit into those old jeans, being able to run for the bus (and catch it!), looking and feeling more confident, feeling less breathless, getting your blood cholesterol down so you don't need tablets, and so on. Think about what this new lifestyle, physique, and so on, will do for you. How will a new image affect other areas of your life – your confidence, your work performance, your social life, your belief in yourself? And how will it affect the way in which you interact with others – family, friends, and colleagues?

If you are absolutely clear about why you would like a healthier lifestyle, you will vastly increase your motivation and therefore, your chances of success.

A practical approach

Follow the nutritional guidelines in this book to help you achieve a balanced intake of the right types of foods. Start by making a note of exactly what you're eating (a food diary), so that you have a written record of days when perhaps things could have gone better. If you couple this with notes about how you were feeling at that particular time, a connection may begin to emerge between your moods and the times when you indulge. This can be useful in helping you to make lasting changes.

There's no need to cook separately for yourself. The best part about eating the right foods for slimming is that they're also great foods for the whole family. Simply serve yourself smaller portions and fill up on the vegetables and starchy foods. Don't skip meals, as this often makes you ravenous by the next meal and you're more likely to overdo it, or to snack on high-Calorie foods in between. A healthy diet, tailored to your own individual needs, may not sound as revolutionary as some of the "miracle" diets endorsed by celebrities, but the evidence shows that it is the best way of losing weight sensibly and keeping it off. Registered dietitians can assess your current eating habits and lifestyle, and advise you on appropriate strategies to lose weight slowly but steadily.

Think slim

✳ Often, keeping to a food plan means that you focus so much on food, that you forget about the benefits of physical activity. Find ways of making exercise a part of your daily life in order to lose weight more quickly. Go for a brisk walk with a friend, splash around in the swimming pool, or work out at the gym. Or, if you find it hard to make time for exercise, try running up and down the stairs at work a few times a day; or at home, jog on the spot while watching your favorite soap.

✳ If you find yourself battling with food cravings, you have two choices: either eat a small amount, enjoy it, and move on, getting quickly back on track. Or, think about how much slimmer and fitter you will be if you keep going, and decide that you won't be defeated by a chunk of cake which would probably disappear in seconds and be nothing more than a "quick fix."

✳ Keep a "thoughts" diary. Write down what you eat, when you eat it, and what you were thinking at the time. You might find that the foods you would ideally like to eat less of creep into the menu when you're feeling low, fed up, or bored. An awareness that you fall into this trap at certain times can help you to stay on track by planning ahead. When you feel down, do other things besides eating to pick yourself up – go for a stroll, listen to some music, phone someone for a chat, soak in the bath, read a magazine – anything that you enjoy that will give you more positive thoughts.

✳ Keep an eye on your eating habits. What time do you eat? Do you eat when you're hungry, or because, for example, it's mid-morning and everyone else is munching something. Are you a night-time snacker? If so, you could look at other ways of occupying yourself in the evenings to distract you from food. And if you must eat at night, choose healthier options, such as fruit, raw vegetables with low-fat dips, fromage frais, diet yogurts, two crackers with a sliver of Cheddar cheese, a couple of crispbreads, or a handful of pretzel sticks or popcorn. Eat from a smaller plate to make your meals look bigger.

✳ List all of the benefits that you hope to enjoy when you are fitter and healthier (see page 32). If you catch yourself straying, simply refer to your list and remind yourself of what you could achieve. Keep your list by the fridge, or anywhere eye-catching to keep you motivated.

Get physical

Physical activity helps your body to release endorphins, natural painkillers, which can in turn help you to combat stress and feel more energized. You don't need to jog ten times around the park or go to the gym every day in order to stay fit. Just try to incorporate simple activities into your daily lifestyle and gradually try to work up to 30 minutes a day, five times a week.

✳ Walk to the mailbox, take the dog out more often, take the kids for a brisk walk, or simply park the car a bit farther away from your destination. Try to walk at a pace that leaves you slightly out of breath.

✳ Use the stairs instead of the elevator whenever possible, or run up and down the steps at home a few times a day.

✳ Try skipping or jogging on the spot while watching TV.

✳ Take up a sport that you enjoy and which fits into your routine. Swimming with the kids or salsa dancing classes with a friend is a fun way of working out.

✳ Remember that activity can be therapeutic, so tackling those garden weeds can have more benefits than you think.

And if you feel like giving it all up, take a look at your list of how great you'll feel when you get there, and simply start again. You're human – it's perfectly acceptable to have "off" days.

Keeping healthy – for life

In June 2002, the Diabetes Research and Wellness Foundation launched "Think Well to be Well," a new concept in caring for people with diabetes. Bringing a fresh approach to diet and diabetes, the concept helps people with diabetes to take control of their life and to focus on achieving sustainable results. Let's take a look now at some practical steps based on this concept, which will allow you to challenge your thinking, helping you to achieve more long-term results.

Old habits die hard…
…so they say. But it's actually making that decision to make the change that takes longer. So, start today by changing your attitude and you'll soon find other things changing with it.

What should you say to yourself?
The way you think can have a dramatic effect on your behavior, including what you eat. The instructions that you feed your mind are what the mind will respond to. Practice giving yourself positive reinforcement and encourage-ment. Link these thoughts directly with your goal. For example, say things like, "I feel better about myself when I eat fruit after lunch," or "I'm doing well by walking more." Imagine what others might say to support you, that would give you a positive feeling.

Your mind is programmed to give you more of whatever you are thinking about, so if you're thinking about being fat or unfit, you are inadvertently programming yourself to get what you don't want. Tennis players, for example, know that if they worry about hitting the ball into the net, that is exactly where it is likely to go, so they focus on getting the ball just where they want it to go. The trick is to make conscious choices that bring you closer to your goal, in this case, achieving a healthy lifestyle.

Keeping your diabetes in check

* Quit smoking now.

* Keep to recommended foods most of the time. The more low-GI (see page 12) balanced foods you eat, the better. Choose foods you enjoy and which fit in with your lifestyle, so that any changes are sustainable.

* Make sure you incorporate regular physical activity into your daily habits. This could be as simple as walking up the stairs, or parking the car a little farther away from your destination than normal.

* Keep to your prescribed dose of medication, unless it has been recommended by your medical advisers that you make changes.

* Check your blood glucose regularly so you can assess how your diabetes is at any given time.

* Attend your clinic for regular check-ups, and make sure that you monitor the health of your feet and eyes.

* Take appropriate action during periods of illness, or when going on vacation.

* Keep to within the maximum daily limits of alcohol (see page 23).

* Find ways of relaxing that will help you to combat stress.

Keeping the weight off

So you've done well and reached your desired weight. The last thing you want to do now is to put all that weight back on. But the sad fact is that most people who lose weight do regain it. So how can you make sure that doesn't happen to you? If your weight-reducing diet is something that you simply put up with until you reach your goal, then maybe it's the wrong diet for you. Seeing it as an endurance test is likely to make you indulge when it's over, which tends to make you fall back into those old habits. And then, of course, the weight creeps back on again.

Here are some "think slim" tips:

* Treat your slimming plan as a new way of life. You may lapse occasionally – that's fine. Just acknowledge it and start again.

* Try to keep a sense of perspective about your weight – if you put on a pound or two, you can always take it off again.

* Challenge yourself. Now you have reached your target, what are you going to do next? Why not learn a new sport, or take up a new hobby?

* Find ways to make your work routine and your family support you. You are going to stay slim and healthy.

* Empty out your closets and enjoy giving away clothes that are too big for you. Indulge yourself and buy some new clothes. If you make an effort to look good, you'll want to stay slim.

* Encourage your family and friends to join in with your exercise regime. It's much more fun to go cycling or swimming or play sport with other people.

* Keep a daily "food and mood" diary so you can see when you indulge and what your emotions are up to at that time, e.g., boredom, stress, comfort, security, P.M.T.

* Before you reach for solace in that "unhealthy nibble," ask yourself if choosing this is taking you nearer to the "new" you, and if it isn't, choose again!

* Distract yourself. Perhaps make a creative list of all the things that would work for you, from going for a walk to having a bath or dancing to your favorite CD. By the time you've done this, your brain would have been sufficiently tricked into believing that it no longer needs that "fix"!

from the chef

For the past seven years, I've felt on top of the world. Memories of bronchitis, flu, colds, and coughs had been dispatched by my new love of eating well and eating organic. Visits to the doctor were few and far between and I was starting to feel as if I was untouchable by disease or ailment.

All until I agreed to appear in a TV program about sugar that involved having a test for Syndrome X (see page 9). I must have been mad – the things you do for telly! – but I knew a test this thorough was not available on the National Health Service. It was a complicated drawn-out test where glucose and insulin was pumped into my left arm, and my right arm was placed in an "oven" at 149°F. Blood was taken from it every 10 minutes for two hours, and was then spun centrifugally to test my insulin resistance.

Shock, horror – I had Syndrome X; I was on my way to type 2 diabetes unless, that is, I took steps to change my lifestyle. With Syndrome X, there is a way back, however, unlike with type 2.

It is estimated that between 20 and 25 percent of the UK population has Syndrome X and they won't know a thing about it until it moves on to type 2 diabetes, and that will happen unless you take the right steps. Have a good look at your diet, engage in aerobic exercise to increase your heart rate for at least 20 minutes, four times a week, lose some of those pounds of flesh that seem to have come from nowhere, and, if you smoke, stop.

I have changed my lifestyle and hopefully I won't move on to the diabetes stage, but if I do, then I'm determined still to enjoy my food. Wholesale changes aren't necessary; you can still eat normally – it's just that certain foods need restricting – or if instructed by your doctor, cutting out altogether. But this doesn't mean your diet has to be boring. With a little imagination and a good knowledge of the dos, don'ts, whys, and wherefores, life shouldn't really have to change that much. Although I have written this book for people with diabetes, there is no harm in everyone getting into it, too. Many of us watch what we eat, so there is no reason why you shouldn't have a lifestyle change straight away; an AWT (Antony Worrall Thompson) meal a day may well keep Syndrome X away.

I'll be honest: out of choice I wouldn't use artificial sweeteners that contain aspartame, but natural substitutes for sugar are slowly finding their way on to the market. Even with Syndrome X, I prefer not to use margarines or spreads containing trans fats or hydrogenated vegetable oils since there is more and more evidence that these can harm your health, but there are recipes in this book where there is no substitute. And I won't encourage you to drink artificially sweetened colas for the same reason, since you should try to discover more natural drinks. You can help yourself without reverting to science; natural foods, unenhanced with chemicals, are always going to be a better choice.

None of my recipes requires rocket science. Here are simple "normal" recipes using a little knowledge and a lot of imagination to keep you enjoying your food. There is no regime, just common sense; no sergeant major barking orders, just foodie pleasure. Azmina has already explained the best balance of foods to eat. Remember that each meal should contain vegetables and starchy carbohydrates. Follow Azmina's advice and you'll soon realize that being diagnosed with diabetes need not be a trial or a long-term foodie prison sentence. Life is for living, so give yourself that chance.

breakfasts and brunches

asparagus, smoked bacon and scallion hash

Perfect for a late brunch or lazy lunch, this classic dish combines great flavors with great textures.

1 garlic clove, finely chopped
2 scallions, sliced into 1-inch pieces
2 ounces lean smoked bacon, diced (about ½ cup)
½ tablespoon rapeseed (canola) oil
1 teaspoon capers, drained and rinsed
8 cooked asparagus spears, cut into 2-inch pieces
1 tablespoon black olives, pitted and diced
1 tablespoon balsamic vinegar
3 eggs
Freshly ground black pepper

Serves 2

In a non-stick pan, fry the garlic, scallions, and bacon in the oil until golden. Add the capers, asparagus, olives, and vinegar, and heat through.

Whisk the eggs and pour into the asparagus mix. Stir until the eggs are cooked to your liking, and take on a scrambled appearance.

Season with black pepper to taste and serve on whole-grain toast.

PER SERVING:
203 CALORIES, 14G FAT, 4G SATURATED FAT, 3G CARBOHYDRATE, 0.83G SODIUM

salmon and kipper kedgeree

A pleasant alternative to the usual smoked haddock version. Traditionally a recipe served at breakfast, this also makes a great light lunch, but eat once a week or so, rather than everyday.

1 kippered herring fillet
6-ounce salmon fillet
1 bay leaf
1 cup brown rice
½ onion, chopped
2 tablespoons unsalted butter
2 teaspoons curry paste
2 eggs, hard-boiled and chopped
2 tablespoons chopped parsley
Freshly ground black pepper

Serves 2

Cook the kipper and salmon in two and a half cups water, along with the bay leaf, over medium heat for seven minutes, then let cool slightly. Discard the bay leaf and lift the fish out of the water, reserving the water. Flake the fish, discarding any skin or bone.

Rinse the rice, then measure one cup rice to three cups reserved fish cooking water into a pan, topping up with plain water, if necessary. Bring to a boil, reduce the heat, and simmer covered, for about 30 minutes. Drain, separate the grains with a fork, and set aside.

Meanwhile, cook the onion slowly in the butter until soft but not browned, add the curry paste, and stir to combine. Add the rice, flaked fish, hard-boiled eggs, and parsley, and stir. Season with black pepper to taste and serve immediately.

PER SERVING:
766 CALORIES, 40G FAT, 12G SATURATED FAT, 64G CARBOHYDRATE, 0.73G SODIUM

scrambled eggs and smoked salmon timbales

A classic dish, but given a more chef-style presentation. Two ingredients that combine to make the perfect breakfast.

Rapeseed (canola) oil spray (see page 17)
4 ounces smoked salmon (lox), thinly sliced (about ²/₃ cup)
4 eggs
2 teaspoons horseradish
2 teaspoons chopped chives
Freshly ground black pepper
1 tablespoon unsalted butter
Watercress, for garnishing
Lemon wedges, for garnishing

Serves 2

Lightly spray four timbales (high-sided molds) with oil and line with plastic wrap.

Line each timbale with strips of smoked salmon, making sure there are no gaps, and leaving an overhang to create a lid once the timbales are filled with scrambled eggs.

Lightly beat the eggs, folding in the horseradish and chives, but keeping some viscosity or stickiness (in other words, don't overbeat). Season with pepper.

Melt the butter in a non-stick frying pan or saucepan until it foams, then pour in the eggs. With a wooden spoon, draw the edges of the eggs into the center continuously until they have cooked to your liking. Immediately spoon the scrambled eggs into the smoked salmon molds, push the eggs down with a teaspoon, then fold over the smoked salmon to enclose. Turn the molds out into the center of two plates and garnish with any excess smoked salmon, the watercress, and lemon wedges.

PER SERVING:
277 CALORIES, 18G FAT, 6G SATURATED FAT, 2G CARBOHYDRATE, 1.22G SODIUM

baked egg in herbed roast beefsteak tomato

Eggs with inspiration. A wonderfully rich and filling dish, and the dash of vermouth gives it a touch of decadence.

2 ounces button mushrooms, finely chopped (about ¹/₂ cup)
1 small onion, finely chopped
¹/₂ teaspoon soft thyme leaves
¹/₂ teaspoon ground black pepper
1 tablespoon olive oil
1 tablespoon dry vermouth
4 beefsteak tomatoes
5 eggs
2 tablespoons plain yogurt
2 teaspoons chopped chives
2 teaspoons finely chopped flat-leaf parsley
Freshly ground black pepper

Serves 4

In a saucepan, cook the mushrooms, onion, thyme, and black pepper in the olive oil over gentle heat for about 15 minutes, stirring regularly until the onions have softened and the vegetables have released most of their liquid. Add the vermouth and boil until all the liquid has evaporated, then set aside to keep warm.

Preheat the oven to 350°F. Cut a half inch from the rounded end of each tomato. Hollow out the seeds and discard them. Place the tomatoes, cut side up, on a roasting tray and cook for 10 minutes in the oven, with the lids placed separately on the roasting tray.

Meanwhile, beat one of the eggs. Whisk together the yogurt, herbs, a tablespoon of water, and the beaten egg. Remove the tomatoes from the oven and place a quarter of the mushroom mix in the bottom of each hollowed-out tomato. Break a raw egg on to the mushroom mix, spoon the yogurt mix over the egg, and top each tomato with a tomato lid. Return to the oven and cook for 10–15 minutes, depending on how well you like your eggs cooked.

PER SERVING:
161 CALORIES, 11G FAT, 3G SATURATED FAT, 6G CARBOHYDRATE, 0.11G SODIUM

scrambled crab

Eggs and crab make an excellent partnership and a more unusual combination than scrambled eggs and salmon. White crabmeat comes from the claw of the crab and is the tastiest.

4 eggs
4 ounces white crabmeat (about ½ cup)
Freshly ground black pepper
2 slices whole-grain bread
1 tablespoon unsalted butter
2 tablespoons plain yogurt

Serves 2

Lightly beat the eggs, then combine with the crabmeat. Season with ground black pepper. Toast the bread and spread with half of the butter. Keep warm.

Heat the remaining butter in a non-stick frying pan, pour in the eggs, and stir until cooked to how you like your eggs. Fold in the yogurt, and spoon on to the buttered toast.

PER SERVING:
337 CALORIES, 19G FAT, 7G IS SATURATED FAT, 15G CARBOHYDRATE, 0.55G SODIUM

brown soda bread

This is the easiest bread in the world to make. An Irish specialty, it is raised with baking soda and an acid: the sour milk or buttermilk, instead of yeast.

2 cups lowfat milk or buttermilk
Juice of 1 lemon (if using plain milk)
2½ cups all-purpose white flour
1 rounded teaspoon salt (optional)
1 rounded teaspoon baking soda
2½ cups stone-ground whole wheat flour

Makes 1 loaf

Preheat the oven to 450°F.

To sour the lowfat milk, pour it into a large pitcher, along with the lemon juice. Let stand for 15 minutes to thicken before stirring. If you prefer, you can use buttermilk instead of souring the milk yourself.

Sift the white flour, salt (if using), and baking soda, then add the whole wheat flour, stirring to combine in a large bowl. Make a well in the center and add the soured milk or buttermilk, little by little. Working from the center, combine the mixture either by hand or with a wooden spoon, adding more soured milk if necessary. The dough should be soft, but not sticky. If it becomes too wet, add more flour.

Turn out on to a floured board and knead lightly, just enough to shape into a round loaf. Flatten slightly to about two inches thick and place on a baking tray.

Using a floured large knife, mark a deep cross on top and bake in the oven for 15–20 minutes, then reduce the heat to 400°F for 20–25 minutes, or until the bread is cooked and the bottom sounds hollow when tapped.

PER QUARTER LOAF:
508 CALORIES, 4G FAT, 2G SATURATED FAT, 105G CARBOHYDRATE, 0.75G SODIUM

dried cherry muffins

Other dried fruit can be substituted, but I think that cherries are the most delicious. These muffins are great for a quick breakfast or mid-morning snack.

$^2/_3$ cup lowfat milk or buttermilk
1 tablespoon lemon juice
  (if using plain milk)
Rapeseed (canola) oil spray
  (see page 17)
½ cup dried pitted cherries
1$^1/_4$ cups all-purpose flour

1½ teaspoons baking powder
$^1/_4$ cup (½ stick) unsalted butter
$^1/_3$ cup sugar
1 egg
½ teaspoon grated orange peel

Makes 12 small muffins

Preheat the oven to 350°F.

If using the lowfat milk, combine it with the lemon juice and let stand for 30 minutes. Lightly spray a 12-cup muffin pan or 12 paper muffin cups with oil.

If you have time, soak the cherries in the milk mixture or buttermilk for 30 minutes. I know it's breaking the rules and isn't essential, but it does help to soften the cherries.

In a large bowl, sift together the flour and baking powder. In a separate bowl, cream together the butter and sugar until light and fluffy. Lightly beat the egg, then add to the creamed butter, along with the orange peel, and combine.

Make a well in the center of the flour and baking powder, and spoon in the cherries and soured milk or buttermilk. Add the butter mixture and mix the whole thing together with your hands until just combined. Don't overwork the batter.

Heap the mixture into the muffin cups, filling them two-thirds full. Bake in the oven for about 20 minutes, or until a skewer or toothpick inserted into the center comes out clean. Transfer the muffins to a wire rack to cool.

PER MUFFIN:
131 CALORIES, 5G FAT, 3G SATURATED FAT, 22G CARBOHYDRATE, 0.09G SODIUM

honey, orange, and thyme bran muffins

There is plenty of fiber, but very little fat in these delicious muffins. Wheat bran is available from good healthfood stores.

$^2/_3$ cup lowfat milk or buttermilk
1 tablespoon lemon juice
  (if using plain milk)
Rapeseed (canola) oil spray
  (see page 17)
2 tablespoons soft light
  brown sugar
2 tablespoons unsalted
  butter, melted
2 eggs, lightly beaten

½ teaspoon soft thyme leaves
$^1/_4$ cup honey
Grated peel of 2 oranges
2 cups all-purpose flour
8 ounces unrefined wheat bran
  (about 2 cups)
1 tablespoon baking powder
Pinch of salt

Makes 12 muffins

If using the plain milk, combine it with the lemon juice and let it stand for 30 minutes.

Lightly spray a 12-cup muffin pan or 12 paper muffin cups with oil.

Place the sugar in a bowl and combine with the melted butter, soured milk or buttermilk, eggs, thyme, honey, and orange peel.

In another bowl, combine the flour, bran, baking powder, and salt. Make a well in the dry ingredients and then fold in the milk mixture. Combine until just mixed, but don't overwork the batter.

Fill each muffin cup two-thirds full with the batter and bake for 20–25 minutes until golden and cooked through. To test, insert a skewer into the center of a muffin: if it comes out clean, the muffin is cooked. Remove from the oven, let stand for 10 minutes, then turn the muffins out on to a wire rack to cool completely.

PER MUFFIN:
161 CALORIES, 4G FAT, 2G SATURATED FAT, 27G CARBOHYDRATE, 0.24G SODIUM

2

soups and salads

Jerusalem artichoke soup

Jerusalem artichokes have nothing to do with Jerusalem or artichokes, but are a good part of a healthy diet. They also taste great raw and grated over salads.

Olive-oil spray (see page 17)
1 pound Jerusalem artichokes, peeled, diced, and submerged in acidulated water (water with a little lemon juice or vinegar added)
1 onion, diced
8 ounces floury potatoes, diced (about 1½ cups)
2 garlic cloves, finely chopped
1 celery stalk, diced
1 heaped teaspoon soft fresh thyme leaves
4 cups chicken or vegetable stock
²/₃ cup skim milk
¹/₄ cup plain yogurt
Pinch of freshly grated nutmeg
2 ounces tender young spinach leaves (a large handful)
Freshly ground black pepper

Serves 4

Lightly spray a pot with olive oil. Drain the artichokes and add them to the pan. Add the onion, potatoes, garlic, celery, and thyme, then stir to combine. Cover with a lid and cook for 10 minutes, shaking the pan occasionally, until the potatoes have started to soften but not color.

Pour the stock into the pot, bring to a boil, then reduce to a simmer and cook for another 10 minutes or so until all the vegetables have softened and are completely tender. Let cool a little and then blend it in batches using a hand-held mixer or food processor, until smooth. If you would like a squeaky-smooth soup, put the soup through a food mill. Return the soup to the pot.

Add the milk and yogurt to the pot, whisk to combine, then add the nutmeg and spinach and reheat gently, stirring, until the spinach has wilted. Season with black pepper to taste and ladle into warmed soup bowls. Serve at once with crusty whole-grain bread.

PER SERVING:
164 CALORIES, 2G FAT, 1G SATURATED FAT, 32GCARBOHYDRATE, 0.39G SODIUM

watercress and potato soup

A classic French combination that tastes wonderful and also does you good. This is warm and thick soup, perfect for the winter months.

2 shallots, finely diced
1 sprig thyme
2 tablespoons unsalted butter
2 bunches watercress, leaves and stalks separated
12 ounces floury potatoes, diced (about 2¹/₄–2³/₄ cups)
5 cups vegetable or chicken stock, boiling
¹/₄ cup low-fat yogurt
Freshly ground black pepper

Serves 4

In a pot, cook the shallots and thyme gently in the butter until softened but not colored. Tie the watercress stalks together with string, then put in the pot. Add potatoes and stir to combine.

Add the boiling stock and cook aggressively until the potatoes are soft. Remove the watercress stalks and discard. Add half the watercress leaves, cook for a further minute, then puree in a blender. Pass the puréed soup through a fine mesh strainer. Whisk in the yogurt and the remaining watercress leaves. Heat through and season with black pepper before serving.

PER SERVING:
123 CALORIES, 6G FAT, 3G SATURATED FAT, 13G CARBOHYDRATE, 0.43G SODIUM

cold pea and mint soup with a fava bean salad

A perfect light summer lunch. Use fresh shelled peas when in season, but to be honest, frozen peas are just as nutritious.

4 cups vegetable stock
1 garlic clove, crushed
4 scallions, sliced
1 tablespoon vegetable oil
4 cups shelled peas (fresh or frozen)
1 tablespoon sugar
2 tablespoons chopped fresh mint leaves
Freshly ground black pepper
$^2/_3$ cup plain yogurt

For the fava bean salad
1½ cups fava beans, measured after shelling and skinning, or 14 ounces canned white beans, drained
4 scallions, finely sliced
1 tablespoon olive oil
1 teaspoon lemon juice
1 tablespoon grated Parmesan cheese

Serves 4

In a pot, bring the vegetable stock to a boil.

In separate pot, cook the garlic and scallions in the vegetable oil until the onion is soft but not brown. Add the peas and sugar, then add the boiling stock. Cook for 12 minutes if you are using fresh peas, four minutes if frozen. Let cool.

In a blender, puree the soup with the mint. Season with black pepper to taste, cool, and then refrigerate. When chilled, whisk in the yogurt.

To make the salad, just before serving, combine the fava beans (or white beans) and scallions with the olive oil and lemon juice. Season with plenty of ground pepper. Fold in the Parmesan.

Make a small pile of the salad in the center of four soup plates, pour the soup around the salad, and serve immediately.

PER SERVING:
238 CALORIES, 11G FAT, 3G SATURATED FAT, 22G CARBOHYDRATE, 0.35G SODIUM

a warming rustic garlic soup

A soup to lift the heart, garlic is full of beneficial properties. It is antibacterial, and antiviral and may help to reduce blood cholesterol and nasal congestion.

5 garlic cloves, thinly sliced
1 ounce lean bacon, finely diced (optional) –about $^1/_4$ cup
1 red chile, finely sliced
1 onion, finely sliced
1 teaspoon soft fresh thyme leaves
1 tablespoon olive oil
4 thick slices whole-grain bread, crusts removed
½ teaspoon paprika
2½ cups chicken stock
Freshly ground black pepper

Serves 2

In a pot, cook the garlic, bacon, if using, chile, onion, and thyme in the olive oil until golden. Break the bread into small cubes and add to the pan along with the paprika and chicken stock.

Bring to a boil and simmer for 10 minutes, stirring from time to time until the bread has broken down and thickened the liquid. For a smoother soup, puree in a blender or food processor. Season with black pepper to taste.

PER SERVING:
271 CALORIES, 8G FAT, 1G SATURATED FAT, 42G CARBOHYDRATE, 0.83G SODIUM

toasted pasta in wild mushroom broth

This is the perfect soup to make in autumn or winter when wild mushrooms are at their best. A good source of carbohydrates.

4 ounces whole wheat fettuccine (about 1 cup)
1 tablespoon olive oil
Olive-oil spray (see page 17)
1 teaspoon soft fresh thyme leaves
1 teaspoon chopped garlic
2 onions, roughly chopped
1 ounce dried cèpes or porcini mushrooms, soaked in 1¼ cups boiling water

1 bunch parsley, leaves and stalks
1 teaspoon black peppercorns
5 cups vegetable or chicken stock
8 ounces mixed fresh wild mushrooms, cleaned
2 ounces button mushrooms, cleaned (about ½ cup)
Freshly ground pepper
1 bunch scallions, sliced

Serves 4

Preheat the oven to 350°F.

Break the pasta into smaller pieces, toss in the oil, and place on a baking sheet. Bake in the oven for 10 minutes until golden. Set aside to cool.

Spray a pot with a little olive oil and cook the thyme, garlic, and onions over medium heat for about 10 minutes or until the onion has softened, but not colored. Add the soaked dried mushrooms along with their liquid, the parsley stalks, the peppercorns and the stock, bring to a boil and cook for 30 minutes.

Meanwhile remove any stalks from the wild mushrooms and add them to the stock. Slice the mushroom caps, quarter the button mushrooms, and set aside.

Strain the stock, wipe out the pot, and return the strained liquid to the pot. Add the pasta and the prepared fresh mushrooms, and cook for a further 10 minutes. Season with black pepper to taste and sprinkle with scallions. Serve very hot.

PER SERVING:
184 CALORIES, 5G FAT, 1G SATURATED FAT, 30G CARBOHYDRATE, 0.47G SODIUM

tomato water

The ultimate slimming soup, this is also highly refreshing and light, and well worth the effort. Presentation is everything here: the basil should float elegantly around the small tomato dice.

2¼ pounds ripe but firm vine tomatoes, roughly chopped
1 tablespoon Worcestershire sauce
1 teaspoon Tabasco sauce
½ English cucumber, cut into chunks
1¼ cups Evian water
1 teaspoon salt
3 plum tomatoes, seeded and diced
6 basil leaves

Serves 4

Blend all the ingredients, except for the plum tomatoes and basil, in a blender.

Pour the pulp into jelly bags (or cheesecloth-lined strainer) and let drip through, preferably overnight. Do not force through as this will cloud the liquid. Chill until ready to serve.

Garnish each bowl with diced tomato and some chiffonade of shredded basil. Pour the tomato water over, and serve immediately.

PER SERVING:
64 CALORIES, 1G FAT, 0.1G SATURATED FAT, 12G CARBOHYDRATE, 0.59G SODIUM

grilled shellfish gazpacho

An exciting variation on a Spanish theme; gazpacho is usually a vegetarian soup, but here I have added shrimp, scallops, and crabmeat.

1 slice whole-grain country bread, crusts removed and broken into small chunks
2 teaspoons sherry vinegar
½ garlic clove, finely chopped
1 teaspoon sugar
½ red chile, seeded, finely diced
2 tablespoons olive oil, plus extra for brushing
12 ounces plum tomatoes, peeled and seeded (about 1¼–1½ cups)
1 cup tomato juice
4½ ounces scallions, finely sliced

½ red pepper, roasted or broiled, peeled, seeded, and diced
½ large English cucumber, peeled, seeded, and roughly diced
2 teaspoons pesto
Freshly ground black pepper
3 large raw shrimp, shelled
4 diver-caught scallops, shucked
Basil leaves, for garnishing
4½ ounces white crabmeat
For the basil salt (optional)
Handful of basil leaves
½ cup sea salt

Serves 4

Place the bread in a blender. While blitzing the bread, add the vinegar, garlic, sugar, and chile, and blend until smooth.

Add the olive oil, a little at a time, until it has been absorbed by the bread. Add the tomatoes, tomato juice, scallions, red pepper, cucumber, and pesto. Continue to blitz until a smooth emulsion is formed. Season to taste with black pepper.

To make the basil salt, place the ingredients in a food processor and blend until smooth and green. Store in an airtight container. Half an hour before serving, sprinkle the shrimp and scallops with ½ teaspoon of the basil salt, if desired, and toss to combine.

Dust off the salt from the shrimp and scallops, and brush with a little olive oil. Cook them under a hot broiler or in a grill pan or heavy frying pan for one to two minutes on each side. Ideally, serve in large-rimmed shallow soup bowls. Place the shrimp and scallops in the center, then pour the soup around the shellfish. Scatter each bowl with basil leaves and fresh crab, and serve immediately.

PER SERVING:
198 CALORIES, 10G FAT, 2G SATURATED FAT, 11G CARBOHYDRATE, 0.65G SODIUM

poached shellfish in Asian broth

Another seafood speciality, this soup contains light, vibrant flavors, but with a little bite. A recipe with lots of Asian tastes.

1 tablespoon vegetable oil
1 teaspoon Thai red curry paste
2 garlic cloves, sliced
1 onion, thinly sliced
½ fennel head, thinly sliced
1 tablespoon tomato paste
1 lemongrass stalk, finely chopped
2 dried bird's eye chiles
1 kaffir lime leaf, shredded (optional)
½-inch piece of fresh ginger root, finely chopped
1 "petal" broken off a star anise
9 cups fish stock
1 teaspoon chopped fresh tarragon

For finishing the broth
4 ounces asparagus tips (about 1 cup)
½ cup shelled peas (fresh or frozen)
4 large diver-caught scallops
4 ounces salmon fillet, cut into 4 pieces
8 large shelled shrimp, peeled and de-veined
24 mussels, cleaned
4 ounces white crabmeat (about ½ cup)
3 ounces sugar-snap peas (about 1 handful)
2 tomatoes, quartered and seeded
Juice of 2 limes
1 tablespoon nam pla (Thai fish sauce)
24 cilantro leaves
Handful of baby spinach leaves

Serves 4

Heat the oil in a saucepan, add the curry paste, and cook for a minute, stirring regularly. Add the garlic, onion, and fennel, and cook gently for 10 minutes.

Stir in the tomato paste, lemongrass, chiles, lime leaf (if using), ginger, and star anise. Pour in the stock and add the tarragon. Simmer over low heat for an hour, then strain the broth into a clean saucepan.

Bring the broth to a boil, add the asparagus and peas, and cook for two minutes. Add the scallops and salmon, and cook for a further two minutes. Add the remaining ingredients and cook until the mussels have opened. Ladle into four warm bowls.

PER SERVING:
241 CALORIES, 9G FAT, 1G SATURATED FAT, 10G CARBOHYDRATE, 1.26G SODIUM

a thai soup of whiting and squid

Whiting is an underused fish that is suited to Thai flavors. If you can't find it, you can use cod, haddock, or monkfish instead.

6 cups fish stock
1 lime, thinly sliced
2 kaffir lime leaves, finely shredded
3 garlic cloves, crushed
3 red chiles, thinly sliced
1-inch piece of fresh ginger root, sliced
1 lemongrass stalk, finely chopped
2 tablespoons nam pla (Thai fish sauce)
1 pound whiting fillets, cut into 2-inch cubes
8 ounces baby asparagus tips (about 2 cups)
4 scallions, sliced
1 pound squid tubes, cut into 2-inch squares
6 ounces sugar-snap peas (a very large handful)
Freshly ground black pepper
2 tablespoons chopped cilantro

Serves 6

In a large pot, bring the stock to a boil and add the lime, lime leaves, garlic, chiles, ginger, lemongrass, and nam pla. Simmer for five minutes.

Add the whiting, asparagus, and scallions, and cook for a further four minutes. Then add the squid and peas and cook for just one more minute. Season with black pepper, garnish with the cilantro, and serve immediately.

PER SERVING:
159 CALORIES, 2G FAT, 0.1G SATURATED FAT, 5G CARBOHYDRATE, 0.83G SODIUM

chicken noodle soup

This version of a classic Chinese soup uses buckwheat noodles instead of egg noodles. As the soup contains plenty of carbs, it is best eaten as a main meal.

8 ounces buckwheat noodles
1 teaspoon sesame oil
1 teaspoon vegetable oil
$1/2$ teaspoon grated fresh ginger root
1 garlic clove, finely chopped
$1/2$ teaspoon diced chile
3 scallions, sliced
$1/4$ cup reduced-salt soy sauce
2 teaspoons honey
5 cups chicken stock
Freshly ground black pepper
6 ounces cooked chicken, shredded (about $3/4$-1 cup)
1 tablespoon chopped cilantro

Serves 4

Cook the noodles in boiling water until tender: this should take about four minutes. When the noodles are cooked, drain, and refresh in cold water.

Meanwhile, in a pot, heat both the oils over medium heat. Add the ginger, garlic, chile, and scallions, and cook for three minutes, stirring constantly. Add the soy sauce, honey, and chicken stock, then bring to a boil and simmer for three minutes. Season with black pepper to taste.

Add the noodles to the soup, then add the cooked chicken and cilantro. Reheat for two minutes before serving.

PER SERVING:
326 CALORIES, 7G FAT, 1G SATURATED FAT, 47G CARBOHYDRATE, 1.06G SODIUM

jewelled couscous

Usually an accompaniment to a Moroccan tagine, but it makes a delicious salad, too. A version can also be made with rice. Either way, it is a light and colorful dish, rich in flavors.

1 cup chicken or vegetable stock
1 tablespoon olive oil
½ teaspoon salt
²/₃ cup couscous
Finely grated peel of
1 unwaxed lemon
Juice of ½ lemon
3 tablespoons slivered almonds, toasted
¹/₃ cup dried apricots, soaked in a little water for 20 minutes, drained, and chopped
2 tablespoons golden or regular raisins
¹/₄ cup roughly chopped flat-leaf parsley
¹/₄ cup roughly chopped cilantro

Serves 2

Heat the stock in a large pot with the olive oil and the salt. Bring to a boil and immediately remove from the heat. Pour in the couscous in a thin, steady stream and then stir in the lemon peel. Set aside for 10 minutes to let the grains swell, until the couscous has soaked up all of the liquid.

Return the couscous to the heat and drizzle the lemon juice over it. Heat gently for about five minutes, stirring with a long-pronged fork to fluff up the grains, then remove from the heat.

Fold in the almonds, apricots, raisins, parsley, and cilantro. Season with black pepper to taste. Serve with Chicken Tagine (see page 115) or let cool to room temperature and serve as a healthy salad.

PER SERVING:
343 CALORIES, 14G FAT, 1G SATURATED FAT, 49G CARBOHYDRATE, 0.64G SODIUM

butternut squash salad with garlic, chile, and caraway

Squashes are a good source of beta-carotene and vitamin E. They can be used in sweet or savory dishes and are often cooked with spices.

1 medium-sized butternut squash, cut into wedges
6 garlic cloves
Freshly ground black pepper
1 teaspoon thyme leaves
2 tablespoons olive oil
1 tablespoon balsamic vinegar
1 tablespoon red wine vinegar
1 tablespoon harissa (chile sauce)
1½ teaspoons ground caraway seeds
2 tablespoons chopped cilantro
2 eggs, hard-boiled, peeled and quartered

Serves 4

Preheat the oven to 350°F.

Place the squash in a roasting dish, cut side up, and add the garlic cloves. Sprinkle the squash with pepper and half the olive oil. Roast for about 40 minutes or until soft and golden, turning over from time to time. Remove from the oven and let cool to room temperature.

Scrape the squash pulp from the skin and mash the pulp, along with the garlic and any juices from the roasting dish. Fold in the remaining ingredients except for the eggs.

Place in a bowl and garnish with the eggs before serving.

PER SERVING:
157 CALORIES, 10G FAT, 2G SATURATED FAT, 12G CARBOHYDRATE, 0.06G SODIUM

salsa verde

A light, refreshing side dish, this also makes a great accompaniment to meat dishes such as the Bacon Bollito on page 120. The pickled cucumber, lemon juice, and vinegar give this a surprising kick.

1 handful flat-leaf parsley leaves
6 basil leaves
1 pickled cucumber, roughly chopped
1½ garlic cloves, roughly chopped
1 tablespoon capers, drained and rinsed
2 canned anchovy fillets, drained and rinsed
½ tablespoon red wine vinegar
½ tablespoon lemon juice
3 tablespoons extra virgin olive oil
½ tablespoon Dijon mustard
Pinch of freshly ground black pepper

Serves 4

Coarsely chop together the herbs, pickled cucumber, garlic, capers, and anchovies, or pulse in a food processor. (You get a better result if you hand-chop this salsa.)

Transfer the mixture to a non-reactive bowl and slowly add the remaining ingredients while whisking.

PER SERVING:
87 CALORIES, 9G FAT, 1G SATURATED FAT, 1G CARBOHYDRATE, 0.29G SODIUM

button mushroom and baby spinach salad

A salad with attitude, one for the waistline. This light dish is perfect for summer picnics or as an accompaniment to a main course.

4 ounces button mushrooms (about 1 heaped cup), cleaned and quartered
Pinch of salt
3 tablespoons lemon juice
½ teaspoon ground rosemary
2 tablespoons roughly chopped parsley
2 teaspoons olive oil
3 tablespoons plain yogurt
2 tablespoons skim milk
Freshly ground black pepper
2 handfuls baby spinach
2 tablespoons chopped chives

Serves 2

Place the mushrooms in a large bowl, sprinkle with a little salt, and leave for 30 minutes. Rinse under cold water and dry with paper towels.

Combine the lemon juice, rosemary, parsley, and olive oil, and spoon this over the mushrooms, then toss to combine.

Thin the yogurt with a little milk and pour it over the mushrooms. Season with black pepper to taste.

Divide the spinach between two plates, spoon the mushrooms into the center of the spinach, and sprinkle with the chives.

PER SERVING:
75 CALORIES, 5G FAT, 1G SATURATED FAT, 4G CARBOHYDRATE, 0.48G SODIUM

belgian endive salad with walnuts and croûtons

The slightly bitter taste of the Belgian endive is offset by the nuts and sweet vinegar. Although this is relatively high in fat, most of it is unsaturated.

2 heads Belgian endive
Olive-oil spray (see page 17)
1 garlic clove, diced
1 slice country bread, cut into croûtons
½ tablespoon walnut oil
4 walnuts, roughly chopped
1 tablespoon aged sherry vinegar
Freshly ground black pepper
2 tablespoons chopped chives

Serves 2

Separate the leaves from the endive, and wash if necessary. Retaining a dozen larger whole leaves, shred the remaining endive leaves, then set aside.

Lightly spray a frying pan with olive oil. Heat, then add the garlic and the croûtons and fry until golden. Add the shredded leaves, walnut oil, and walnuts. Cook for one minute and then add the sherry vinegar. Season with black pepper to taste.

Arrange six whole endive leaves around each plate and place the warm chicory salad in the center. Serve immediately.

PER SERVING:
203 CALORIES, 13G FAT, 1G SATURATED FAT, 17G CARBOHYDRATE, 0.14G SODIUM

seared scallops on avocado, beet, and orange salad

Lovely colors, lovely textures, and a little luxury. Choose diver-caught scallops rather than dredged, as dredging damages the sea bed.

Juice and grated peel of 1 orange
Juice and grated peel of 1 lime
1 tablespoon walnut oil
½ tablespoon olive oil
1 shallot, finely diced
Freshly ground black pepper
2 small cooked, but not pickled, beets, cut into ½-inch dice
2 naval oranges, peeled, pith removed, and each sliced horizontally into 5
½ avocado, peeled and diced
4 large diver-caught scallops
Olive-oil spray (see page 17)
2 teaspoons chopped dill

Serves 2

Whisk together the juice and peel of the orange and lime, walnut oil, the olive oil, and shallot, and season with black pepper to taste. Add the beets and leave for a couple of hours until the dressing has taken on a beautiful shade of red.

Arrange half the orange slices on each plate and scatter the diced avocado on top.

Season the scallops with black pepper. Heat a non-stick frying pan over a high flame and lightly spray with olive oil. Add the scallops and cook for one and a half minutes on each side, until crusty and golden, but still a little opaque in the center. Just before serving, spoon the beets with its dressing over the avocado, top each plate with two scallops, and garnish with dill.

PER SERVING:
270 CALORIES, 16G FAT, 2G SATURATED FAT, 19G CARBOHYDRATE, 0.15G SODIUM

spicy sardines with chick pea and avocado salad

A great Mediterranean combo that is just as good made with canned sardines. Sardines and chickpeas are also full of goodness. Serve as a main meal.

Olive-oil spray (see page 17)
1 red chile, diced
2 shallots, diced
1 tablespoon finely chopped
  flat-leaf parsley
1 tablespoon finely
  chopped cilantro
3 garlic cloves, crushed
8 sardines, scaled, cleaned,
  flattened out, and head and
  backbone removed
Juice of 1 lemon

For the chickpea and avocado salad
Yolk of 1 hard-boiled egg
3 tablespoons olive oil
2 tablespoons red wine vinegar
½ red onion, finely chopped
1 garlic clove, crushed
2 tablespoons chopped
  flat-leaf parsley
1 tablespoon small capers,
  drained and rinsed
One 15-ounce can chickpeas,
  drained and rinsed (about 2½ cups)
1 ripe avocado, peeled and
  chopped into chunky dice
Pinch of salt
Freshly ground black pepper

Serves 4

To make the salad, place the egg yolk in a bowl, beat in the oil and vinegar, and stir in the onion, garlic, parsley, capers, chickpeas, and avocado. Season with salt and black pepper.

Preheat the oven to 350°F.

Lightly spray a small frying pan with olive-oil spray, then add the chile and shallots, and cook until softened but not colored. Fold in the parsley, cilantro, and garlic, and season with black pepper, then spread over the flesh side of the fish.

Roll up the sardines and secure with two small wooden toothpicks that have been soaked in water. Cook in the oven for five to eight minutes, then place the sardines on a plate and drizzle with lemon juice. To serve, place a pile of salad on each serving plate and top with two sardine rolls.

PER SERVING:
407 CALORIES, 28G FAT, 4G SATURATED FAT, 13G CARBOHYDRATE, 0.45G SODIUM

mediterranean seafood salad

A special balance of flavors in a healthy package. The Mediterranean diet is one of the healthiest in the world, with its combination of fresh fish, olive oil, and colorful vegetables.

½ cup dry white wine
2¼ pounds mussels, cleaned
6 squid tubes, cut into rings
18 raw tiger shrimp, peeled
6 diver-caught scallops, cut in half
One 6½-ounce can cockles or
  baby clams, shelled and drained
4½ ounces cooked white crabmeat
  (about 1 heaped ½ cup)

3 garlic cloves, crushed
2 red chiles, finely sliced
½ red onion, diced
3 tablespoons olive oil
1 tablespoon lemon juice
Freshly ground black pepper
2 tablespoons chopped parsley
Crisp lettuce

Serves 6

In a large pot, bring the white wine to a boil, add the mussels, cover, and cook for five minutes or until the mussels have opened. Remove the mussels from the pot and set aside, reserving the liquid. Discard any that remain closed. Shell the mussels when cool enough to handle.

In the boiling juices that remain in the pot, cook the squid, shrimp, and scallops for one minute. Remove the fish (do not throw away the cooking liquid), and let the shellfish cool, and combine with the mussels, cockles or clams, and white crabmeat.

Boil the mussel cooking liquid until it has reduced to about a quarter cup. Combine it with the garlic, chiles, onion, olive oil, and lemon juice. Pour the juices over the seafood and toss to combine. Refrigerate for 30 minutes, season with black pepper, and fold in the chopped parsley.

Serve on a bed of crisp lettuce along with some warm crusty whole-grain bread to mop up the juices.

PER SERVING:
243 CALORIES, 9G FAT, 1G SATURATED FAT, 4G CARBOHYDRATE, 0.46G SODIUM

warm salad of asparagus, field mushrooms and peas

Something a little different, this is a wonderful spring dish, when asparagus and fresh peas are in season.

10 medium asparagus spears, trimmed, and peeled if necessary
3 ounces shelled young peas (about $^3/_4$ cup)
2 tablespoons olive oil
1 garlic clove, mashed to a paste
4 field mushrooms, stalks removed, peeled if necessary
Freshly ground black pepper
2 slices whole wheat bread
$^1/_2$ shallot, finely chopped
3 tablespoons dry vermouth (optional)
2 tablespoons low-fat yogurt
$^1/_2$ tablespoon chopped flat-leaf parsley
$^1/_2$ tablespoon chopped chives
$^1/_2$ teaspoon chopped fresh tarragon
$^1/_2$ tablespoon lemon juice
$^1/_2$ handful arugula
$^1/_2$ handful watercress

Serves 2

Cook the asparagus in boiling water for one minute, drain, reserving the cooking water, and set aside.

Add the peas to the asparagus cooking water and cook for two minutes, drain, then set aside.

Prepare your barbecue, broiler, or grill pan.

Combine the olive oil and garlic and brush it over the asparagus and the mushrooms. Season the asparagus and mushrooms with black pepper.

Broil or barbecue the mushrooms for five minutes on each side, and the asparagus for two minutes each side. Keep both warm. Brush both sides of the bread with garlic-infused oil and grill or broil until both sides are toasted.

In a saucepan, heat the remaining garlic oil, add the shallot, and over medium heat let it cook without coloring. Add the dry vermouth, if using, increase the heat, and cook for a further minute. Remove the pan from the heat and whisk in the yogurt, a little at a time. Fold in the peas, parsley, chives, tarragon, and lemon juice. Season to taste. Return to a gentle heat to warm through.

Combine the arugula and watercress and divide between two plates. Top the leaves with a slice of the grilled bread. Divide the asparagus and mushrooms between the bread slices, arranging them attractively on top of each slice. Spoon the peas and juices over the salad leaves.

PER SERVING:
261 CALORIES, 14G FAT, 2G SATURATED FAT, 24G CARBOHYDRATE, 0.22G SODIUM

thai-inspired melon salad

This salad was created as a result of my visits to Thailand. The vibrant flavors go well with melon, creating a refreshing salad with a twist. As this is a salty salad, keep the rest of the day's intake of salt low.

2 garlic cloves, crushed
1 tablespoon honey
2 teaspoons nam pla (Thai fish sauce)
Juice of 2 limes
1 tablespoon grated lime peel
2 red chiles, finely diced
6 ounces cooked and shelled shrimp (about 1 1/2 cup)
1/3 cup unsalted roasted peanuts
1 Galia or Ogen melon, peeled and chopped into 1-inch dice
1/4 cup chopped cilantro
1 tablespoon chopped mint leaves

Serves 4

In a large bowl, combine the garlic, honey, nam pla, lime juice, lime peel and chiles. Fold in the shrimp and peanuts. Add the melon and stir to combine.

Garnish with chopped cilantro and mint. Chill until ready to serve.

PER SERVING:
162 CALORIES, 7G FAT, 1G SATURATED FAT, 10G CARBOHYDRATE, 1.87G SODIUM

shrimp and corn salad

This is the salad for those in a hurry. Just throw it all together in a bowl to create a healthy meal in minutes. Quick, simple, and exceedingly tasty.

1 egg yolk
2 tablespoons olive oil
1 tablespoon lemon juice
1/2 tablespoon Dijon mustard
2 tablespoons plain yogurt
2 tablespoons chopped chives
2 tablespoons chopped dill
1 tablespoon sliced scallion
12 frozen shrimp, cooked
6 ounces fresh or frozen corn, cooked (about 3/4 cup)

Serves 2

Whisk together the egg yolk, oil, lemon juice, and mustard. Once this has emulsified, fold in the yogurt.

Add the herbs and scallion, and combine with the shrimp and corn.

PER SERVING:
426 CALORIES, 19G FAT, 3G SATURATED FAT, 18G CARBOHYDRATE, 1.57G SODIUM

rare tuna salade niçoise

This was inspired by the classic salade niçoise, which uses canned tuna. Fresh tuna, of course, contains lots of beneficial omega-3 fatty oils. Eat as a main course with crusty bread.

2 x 3^1/$_2$-ounce fresh tuna steaks, each ideally 1-inch thick
4 new salad potatoes
2 eggs, at room temperature
2 ounces extra-fine green beans, trimmed (about ^{1}/$_2$ cup)
2 Bibb lettuce hearts, quartered lengthwise and separated
  into leaves
2 plum tomatoes, roughly chopped
^{1}/$_2$ red onion, finely sliced
4 canned anchovy fillets, drained, rinsed, and cut lengthwise
  into thin strips
10 black olives, pitted
8 basil leaves, torn
For the marinade
2 tablespoons olive oil
1 tablespoon aged red wine vinegar
1 tablespoon chopped flat-leaf parsley
1 tablespoon chopped chives
1 garlic clove, finely chopped
Freshly ground black pepper

Serves 2

To make the marinade, place the olive oil, vinegar, parsley, chives, garlic, and a teaspoon of pepper in a bowl, whisking to combine.

Place the tuna in a shallow non-metallic dish and pour half of the marinade over it. Cover with plastic wrap and chill for one hour, to let the flavors penetrate the tuna, turning after about 30 minutes or so.

Place the potatoes in a pan of boiling water, cover, and simmer for 10–12 minutes or until just tender. Drain, then cut into quarters lengthwise.

Place the eggs in a small pan and just cover with boiling water, then cook for six minutes. Drain, and rinse under cold running water, remove the shells, and cut each egg in half; they should still be slightly soft. Plunge the green beans in a pan of boiling water and blanch for three minutes or so, then drain and refresh in cold water.

Heat a grill pan for five minutes. Remove the tuna from the marinade, shaking off any excess. Cook the tuna for about two minutes on each side, depending on how rare you like it.

Arrange the lettuce leaves on serving plates or on one large platter and add the potatoes, green beans, tomatoes, onion, and anchovies. Place the tuna steaks on top and drizzle the remaining marinade over them. Scatter the eggs, olives, and torn basil leaves on top, and serve.

PER SERVING:
442 CALORIES, 25G FAT, 5G SATURATED FAT, 21G CARBOHYDRATE, 0.71G SODIUM

asian chicken salad

With the great flavors of the Orient – papaya, cilantro, mint, chile, and lime – this is a simple salad to make, but full of flavor. Perfect for a light lunch or as an appetizer.

1 pound shredded chicken from "The Really Useful Chicken" recipe (see page 116)
1 carrot, cut into julienne strips
½ green papaya, peeled and cut into julienne strips
3 tablespoons chopped mint
3 tablespoons chopped cilantro
1 bunch scallions, sliced
½ celeriac, cut into julienne strips
¼ cup unsalted peanuts, roughly chopped
Freshly ground black pepper
For the dressing
2 teaspoons finely chopped garlic
1 tablespoon finely chopped chile
²/₃ cup lime juice
2 tablespoons nam pla (Thai fish sauce) or reduced-salt light soy sauce
1 tablespoon honey

Serves 4

To make the dressing, combine the ingredients in a bowl.

In another large bowl, mix the remaining ingredients with enough of the dressing to coat, and season well with black pepper to taste.

PER SERVING:
297 CALORIES, 12G FAT, 3G SATURATED FAT, 12G CARBOHYDRATE, 0.69G SODIUM

asian slaw

A healthier alternative to normal mayonnaise-based coleslaw, this recipe again draws on the delicious tastes of the Far East, where the diet is low in saturated fat, something the Western world would do well to follow.

8 ounces bok choy, shredded (about 3½-4 cups)
5 ounces carrots, cut into julienne strips (about 1 cup)
4 shallots, sliced
½ tablespoon grated fresh ginger root
2 tablespoons shredded basil leaves
2 tablespoons fresh cilantro
1 tablespoon fresh mint leaves
1 garlic clove, chopped
1 hot chile, seeded and finely chopped
Juice and grated peel of
1 orange
Juice of 2 limes
1 tablespoon nam pla (Thai fish sauce)
½ teaspoon sugar
2 tablespoons peanut oil
Freshly ground black pepper
1 tablespoon crushed roasted peanuts

Serves 2

Mix the bok choy in a bowl with the carrots, shallots, ginger, basil, cilantro, mint, garlic, chile, and orange peel.

In a small bowl, whisk together the orange juice, lime juice, nam pla, and sugar. Slowly whisk in the oil until emulsified. Add the dressing to the bok choy and toss well. Season with pepper. Cover and chill for two to six hours.

Just before serving, sprinkle with the crushed roasted peanuts.

PER SERVING:
222 CALORIES, 16G FAT, 3G SATURATED FAT, 16G CARBOHYDRATE, 0.82G SODIUM

3

light meals and appetizers

mushroom "caviar"

An excellent alternative to the usual range of dips, and much healthier. Although the texture may resemble caviar, it has nothing to do with fish or fish roe.

1 tablespoon olive oil
$^1/_2$ onion, finely diced
2 garlic cloves, finely diced
1 teaspoon thyme leaves
4 ounces field mushrooms (e.g., portobello), roughly chopped (about 1 cup)
1 tablespoon balsamic vinegar
Freshly ground black pepper

Serves 4

Heat the oil in a deep saucepan over medium heat. Add the onion, garlic, and thyme, and cook until soft but not brown.

Add the mushrooms, stir to combine, and increase the heat. Cook for 10 minutes, or until the mushrooms have released their liquid. Then add the balsamic vinegar and cook until all the liquid has evaporated. Season with black pepper to taste.

Blend the mixture in a food processor until roughly chopped but not pulverised. Serve warm or at room temperature, with crusty whole-grain bread or oatcakes.

PER SERVING:
39 CALORIES, 3G FAT, 0.4G SATURATED FAT, 3G CARBOHYDRATE, 0G SODIUM

asparagus with red pepper sauce

The red peppers add a natural sweetness to the asparagus, a great partnership, and fantastic combination of colors. Eat as an appetizer or to accompany a main course.

2 red peppers, seeded and roughly chopped
1 onion, roughly chopped
2 garlic cloves, crushed
1 red chile, finely diced
12 basil leaves, plus extra for garnishing
1 tablespoon walnut oil
1 tablespoon sherry vinegar
2 tablespoons lemon juice
11 ounces asparagus, trimmed (about 10–14 spears)
Freshly ground black pepper

Serves 4

Place all the ingredients, except the asparagus, in a large, non-reactive (not aluminum) saucepan, cover, and simmer gently for 20 minutes, stirring from time to time.

Pour the softened pepper mixture into a food processor and blend until smooth. Put through a fine mesh strainer and set aside, keeping it warm, if you wish.

Cook the asparagus in boiling water for six minutes, then drain. Spoon the red pepper sauce (hot or cold) on to four plates and top with the asparagus. Garnish with basil leaves and ground black pepper.

PER SERVING:
79 CALORIES, 4G FAT, 0.3G SATURATED FAT, 9G CARBOHYDRATE, 0.01G SODIUM

bruschetta with white bean purée and raw mushrooms

A much healthier version of a classic dish, this has lots of fiber and even more flavor.

2 tablespoons olive oil
2 garlic cloves, 1 of them finely diced, 1 cut in half
1 teaspoon finely chopped rosemary leaves
One 15-ounce can cannellini beans, rinsed and drained
$2/3$ cup vegetable stock
Freshly ground black pepper
2 ounces button mushrooms, cleaned and sliced
   (about $1/2$ cup)
Juice of $1/2$ lemon
1 tablespoon chopped oregano leaves
4 thick slices whole-grain country bread

Serves 4

In a saucepan, combine one tablespoon of the olive oil, the diced garlic, and the rosemary, and cook over gentle heat until the garlic is soft but without color.

Add the beans and stock, stir to combine, then cook for about 10 minutes. If the mixture dries out too much, add a little more vegetable stock to moisten. Mash with a potato masher or pulse in a food processor to create a rough purée. Season to taste with ground black pepper.

Meanwhile, toss the sliced mushrooms with the remaining olive oil, the lemon juice, oregano, and some black pepper. Broil the bread on both sides and rub with the two garlic halves. Top with the bean purée, then the mushroom mix. Serve with some salad greens.

PER SERVING:
225 CALORIES, 7G FAT, 1G SATURATED FAT, 32G CARBOHYDRATE, 0.36G SODIUM

stewed artichokes with spices and apricots and other things

A wonderfully spicy, nutritious vegetarian stew that is well worth the effort.

4 large artichokes
Juice of 1 lemon, lemon peel reserved
2 garlic cloves, finely sliced
10 black peppercorns
12 coriander seeds, toasted
$1/2$ teaspoon ground turmeric
$1/8$ teaspoon cayenne pepper
$1/2$ teaspoon cumin seeds, toasted
2 onions, cut in eighths
2 bay leaves
$1/4$ cup olive oil
Pinch of saffron strands, soaked in a little cold water
2 carrots, sliced
$2^1/2$ cups vegetable stock
8 dried apricots, sliced
$1/4$ cup raisins
$1/4$ cup almonds, sliced
One 14-ounce can chickpeas, drained and rinsed
8 ounces baby spinach (about $2^1/2$ cups)
2 tablespoons roughly chopped cilantro
$1/4$ cup roughly chopped flat-leaf parsley

Serves 4

Trim the artichokes by peeling the stem until all woody matter has disappeared. Pull off all the tough outer leaves until you reach the pale green ones. Cut off about an inch from the top of the artichoke. Cut the artichoke vertically into four, and cut or pull out the choke. Rub all the cut surfaces with the lemon peel and place the artichoke quarters in a bowl of water. Add the lemon juice.

Using a mortar and pestle or coffee grinder, crush the garlic, peppercorns, coriander seeds, turmeric, cayenne, and cumin seeds.

In a saucepan, cook the onions and bay leaves in the olive oil over medium heat until they have softened but not colored, this should take about eight minutes. Add the spice mixture and cook for a further three minutes.

Add the drained artichokes and the saffron, along with its soaking liquor, and toss to combine. Add the carrots, half the vegetable stock, the apricots, raisins, and almonds, and simmer, covered for about 20 minutes, stirring from time to time. Add more stock as necessary.

When the artichokes are tender, add the chickpeas, spinach, cilantro, and parsley, and stir to combine. Cook until the spinach has wilted. Season with black pepper to taste. Serve hot or cold, with steamed couscous.

PER SERVING:
416 CALORIES, 19G FAT, 2G SATURATED FAT, 46G CARBOHYDRATE, 0.52G SODIUM

stuffed peppers with brandade

A French dish, brandade is made by beating milk, olive oil, and poached fish into a paste. Usually made with salt cod, it works equally well with fresh cod or haddock.

2 potatoes, cut into 1-inch cubes
12 ounces fresh cod
$^2/_3$ cup lowfat milk
2 garlic cloves, crushed
Juice of 1 lemon
2 tablespoons olive oil
$^2/_3$ cup ground almonds (optional)
Freshly ground black pepper
4 drained wood-roasted peppers
Lemon wedges, for serving

Serves 4

Cook the potatoes in water until soft. Mash and set aside. Place the cod in a shallow frying pan, add the milk, and bring to a boil. Remove from the heat and let the cod cool in the milk.

When the cod is cool enough to handle, remove from the milk and flake into a large bowl. Add the garlic, lemon juice, olive oil, and almonds (if using), and combine well. Add the mashed potato to make a fairly thick paste. Season with black pepper to taste.

Stuff each pepper with the brandade paste and serve at room temperature, garnished with lemon wedges.

PER SERVING:
332 CALORIES, 20G FAT, 3G SATURATED FAT, 19G CARBOHYDRATE, 1.28G SODIUM

tortino

This is similar to a frittata or tortilla in that the eggs hold the asparagus and spinach together to make a vegetarian "cake" (colloquially, tortino means cake in Italian). Great for a light meal.

8 ounces asparagus, cut into
1-inch pieces (about 2 cups)
1 shallot, finely diced
1 tablespoon unsalted butter
2 handfuls spinach, thick stems removed
1 teaspoon soft thyme leaves
5 large eggs, beaten
1 tablespoon skim milk
1 tablespoon grated Parmesan, cheese
Freshly ground black pepper

Serves 4

Preheat the oven to 400°F.

Blanch the asparagus in boiling water for three minutes, then refresh in cold water to arrest the cooking. Drain.

Pan-fry the shallot in the butter until softened but not colored, then add the spinach and thyme leaves, and cook until the leaves have wilted. Squeeze the liquid from the spinach and transfer the drained mixture to a lightly buttered shallow baking dish. Place the asparagus on top of the spinach.

Beat the eggs, then combine with the milk and Parmesan. Season with black pepper, and pour on top of the vegetables. Lift the vegetables slightly to let the egg cover the bottom of the dish.

Place in the oven and cook for about 15 minutes or until the eggs are set. This dish can be eaten hot or at room temperature.

PER SERVING:
162 CALORIES, 12G FAT, 4G SATURATED FAT, 2G CARBOHYDRATE, 0.16G SODIUM

salmon and haddock fishcakes

Everybody loves fishcakes and these are particularly good ones, great hot or cold. Serve with the Salsa Verde on page 62.

10 oz. smoked haddock fillets	2 eggs
6 ounces salmon fillets	10 ounces potatoes, cooked and
2½ cups skim milk	mashed (about 1 cup)
1 onion, sliced	2 teaspoons anchovy paste
1 carrot, chopped	2 eggs, hard-boiled, peeled and
1 bay leaf	chopped
1 teaspoon black peppercorns	2 tablespoons chopped parsley
2 cloves	1 tablespoon chopped dill
2 tablespoons olive oil	Freshly ground black pepper
	All-purpose flour
	Fresh whole-grain bread crumbs

Serves 4

Place the haddock and salmon in a large frying pan or flameproof roasting pan. Add enough milk to cover. Add one-third of the onion, the carrot, bay leaf, peppercorns, and cloves. Bring to a boil and then simmer for six minutes. Set aside to cool slightly.

Cut the rest of the onion into dice. Heat half of the olive oil in a pan and briefly sweat the onion until softened, this should take about six to eight minutes.

Remove the fish from the milk and flake the fish, discarding any skin or bones. Strain the liquid and reserve.

Beat one of the eggs. Combine the haddock with the mashed potato, sweated onions, beaten egg, and anchovy paste. Fold in the hard-boiled eggs, parsley, and dill until well combined, but do not over-mix. Season with black pepper to taste. If the mixture is too dry, mix in some of the strained fish liquid. Divide the mixture into four, and shape into patties.

Beat the remaining egg with a little water in a bowl. Season the flour and place on a plate. Place the bread crumbs on another plate. Dip the patties in the flour, the egg, and finally the bread crumbs. Refrigerate for two hours.

Pan-fry the fishcakes in the remaining olive oil for five minutes on each side, and keep warm in the oven.

PER SERVING:
424 CALORIES, 20G FAT, 5G SATURATED FAT, 28G CARBOHYDRATE, 0.91G SODIUM

oriental smoked salmon rolls

Canapés, snacks, brunch – this is perfect for all kinds of occasions. Make sure that the fresh colors of the radish, papaya, and cucumber peek out from the salmon rolls.

1 green papaya, peeled and cut into thin matchsticks
½ English cucumber, peeled and cut into thin matchsticks
8 radishes, thinly sliced
½ cup rice wine vinegar
Juice and peel of 3 limes
1 tablespoon reduced-salt
soy sauce
1 tablespoon honey
6 scallions, finely shredded
12 ounces smoked salmon (lox), cut into long strips (about 2 cups)
48 mint leaves
48 cilantro leaves

Makes 24 rolls

Combine the papaya, cucumber, and radishes in a bowl.

Whisk together the rice wine vinegar, lime juice and peel, soy sauce, and the honey, then pour it over the papaya salad and let stand for two hours. Drain, and fold in the scallions.

Cut the smoked salmon in 3-inch lengths. Place two leaves of each herb on the salmon, top with a little of the pickled vegetables, and roll up tightly. Cover and refrigerate until ready to serve.

PER ROLL:
28 CALORIES, 0.7G FAT, 0.1G SATURATED FAT, 2G CARBOHYDRATE, 0.3G SODIUM

stuffed sardines

This dish has a hint of Moroccan influence, with a filling of nuts and currants. Sardines are a great-tasting oily fish, full of healthy omega-3 fatty acids.

1 red onion, very finely chopped
3 tablespoons olive oil
³/₄ cup fresh whole-grain bread crumbs
5 tablespoons currants, soaked in water for 15 minutes if very dry
3 tablespoons pine nuts
1 bunch parsley, chopped
5 tablespoons mixed lemon and orange juice
Freshly ground black pepper
Olive-oil spray (see page 17)
12 sardines, scaled, cleaned, flattened out, and head and
  backbone removed
¹/₂ lemon, cut into ¹/₄-inch thick slices
¹/₂ orange, cut into ¹/₄-inch thick slices
12 fresh or 6 dried bay leaves, broken in half

Serves 4 as a starter (2 as a main course)

In a saucepan, sweat the onion in the olive oil. Add the bread crumbs and cook for two to three minutes. Remove from the heat and add the currants, pine nuts, and parsley. Pour in the citrus juices and stir. Season with black pepper and mix well.

Let cool.

Preheat the oven to 400°F.

Lightly oil a baking dish with the olive-oil spray. Fill each sardine with one to two teaspoons of filling. Roll each fish from head to tail. Pack the sardines tightly together in the dish with their tails sticking up in the same direction. Sprinkle them with the remaining filling. Place the orange and lemon slices and the bay leaves around the sides of the dish and tucked between the sardines. Bake for 10–15 minutes or until golden. Serve warm or at room temperature.

PER SERVING:
489 CALORIES, 29G FAT, 5G SATURATED FAT, 25G CARBOHYDRATE, 0.23G SODIUM

creamy sardines on toast

Sardines on toast never tasted so good. Canned sardines also contain omega-3 fats and are really versatile pantry-stored food. A great snack.

1 tablespoon olive oil
¹/₂ onion, finely diced
1 teaspoon soft thyme leaves
3 tablespoons whole wheat bread crumbs
²/₃ cup low-fat yogurt
1 small can sardines, drained and mashed
2 eggs, hard-boiled, peeled and chopped
Freshly ground black pepper
2 slices whole-grain bread

Serves 2

Heat the olive oil in a frying pan, add the onion and thyme, and cook until the onion is soft but not brown. Add the remaining ingredients, except the bread, and warm through, stirring to combine. Season with black pepper to taste.

Preheat the broiler. Toast the bread, then share the mixture equally between the slices. Pop under a hot broiler until the mixture bubbles. Serve hot.

PER SERVING:
442 CALORIES, 23G FAT, 5G SATURATED FAT, 29G CARBOHYDRATE, 0.73G SODIUM

a bowl of steaming mussels

Mussels are such good value and this recipe is a variation on the traditional French dish, Moules marinière.

1 tablespoon olive oil
1 onion, finely diced
4 canned anchovy fillets, drained, rinsed and chopped
4 large garlic cloves, chopped
1 red chile, chopped
1 glass white wine (½ cup)
²/₃ cup fish stock
2¹/₄ pounds mussels, cleaned
¹/₄ cup finely chopped parsley
Freshly ground black pepper

Serves 4 as a starter (2 as a main course)

Heat the olive oil in a large pot over medium heat. Add the onion, anchovies, garlic, and chile, and cook until the onion is soft but not brown. Add the wine and the stock, and bring to a boil. Simmer for five minutes, then add the mussels and cover. Increase the heat and cook for approximately five minutes, shaking the pan from time to time.

Remove the mussels with a slotted spoon to warm bowls, discarding any that have not opened.

Boil the remaining liquid for a further two minutes, then add the parsley, and season with ground black pepper. Pour the liquid over the mussels and serve with crusty whole-grain bread.

PER SERVING:
130 CALORIES, 5G FAT, 1G SATURATED FAT, 6G CARBOHYDRATE, 0.39G SODIUM

sardines with tomatoes and red onion

Another great sardine recipe, this makes a delicious light lunch or supper, simple to prepare with ingredients that you will probably have in your cupboard.

1 pound, 2 ounces fresh plum tomatoes, sliced
  (about 2¹/₂–3 cups)
¹/₂ red onion, finely sliced
2 cans of sardines, drained and rinsed
3 pinches of dried oregano
Pinch of dried red chile flakes
Freshly ground black pepper
Balsamic vinegar, to taste
Fresh marjoram leaves
Handful of black olives

Serves 4

Arrange the tomato slices on a serving plate so that they overlap. Scatter with red onion slices. Arrange the sardines carefully over the tomatoes. Sprinkle the sardines with oregano, chile flakes, and freshly ground black pepper.

Drizzle a little balsamic vinegar over the plate. Garnish with some fresh marjoram leaves and black olives. Serve at room temperature.

PER SERVING:
192 CALORIES, 11G FAT, 2G SATURATED FAT, 6G CARBOHYDRATE, 0.47G SODIUM

tuna kabobs with pickled lemon and mint

Great for a barbecue, these kabobs are both tasty and nutritious. Tuna and tomatoes are Mediterranean "musts," especially when combined with sunshine!

4 pickled lemons
1 bunch mint, leaves only
4 garlic cloves, roughly chopped
1/2 teaspoon dried red chile flakes
1 tablespoon olive oil
2 1/4 pounds tuna loin, cut into 16 even-sized cubes
12 bay leaves
12 cherry tomatoes

Serves 4

Cut the pickled lemons in half, scoop out the flesh, and set aside for another use. Cut the rinds of three of the lemons into 12 pieces of roughly even size. Place the rind of the fourth lemon in a food processor along with the mint, garlic, chile flakes, oil, and two tablespoons of water, and pulse until smooth. Spoon into a bowl, then add the tuna pieces and marinate for 20 minutes.

Slide one piece of tuna on to a bamboo skewer that has been soaked in water. Follow the tuna with one bay leaf, one tomato, and one piece of lemon rind. Do this three more times, finishing the kabob with a piece of tuna. Prepare three more skewers in this way.

Preheat the broiler to its highest setting or heat a large frying pan or grill pan. Charbroil the skewers for one minute on each side until they are medium rare, or as you like them. Serve with a green salad.

PER SERVING:
393 CALORIES, 15G FAT, 4G SATURATED FAT, 5G CARBOHYDRATE, 0.52G SODIUM

anchovy toasts

An unusual dish, but it's worth being a little avant-garde for these delicious flavors. Anchovies are usually bought canned, but fresh anchovies are a delicacy in Portugal, Spain, and Turkey.

4 dried figs, roughly chopped
1 tablespoon Pernod
1/4 cup green tea
2 ounces whole almonds, toasted (about 1/3 cup)
1 ounce macadamia nuts (about 1/4 cup)
4 scallions, roughly chopped
2 garlic cloves, roughly chopped
1 teaspoon fresh tarragon leaves
1 teaspoon dill leaves
1 teaspoon flat-leaf parsley
2 sun-dried tomatoes, drained
3 cherry peppers, seeded
Juice and peel of 2 limes
1 tablespoon olive oil
4 slices whole-grain bread, toasted
8 canned anchovy fillets, drained, rinsed, and sliced in half lengthwise

Serves 4 (2 as a main course)

Preheat the oven to 400°F.

Soak the figs in the Pernod and tea for two hours. Combine the figs with the remaining ingredients, except the toast and anchovies.

Spread the fig mixture on the toast and cook in the oven for 10 minutes. Cut each slice into two pieces and top with the anchovy fillets. Eat while hot.

PER SERVING:
315 CALORIES, 18G FAT, 2G SATURATED FAT, 30G CARBOHYDRATE, 0.5G SODIUM

trout in a red pepper blanket

Trout is such an underrated fish, but it is excellent value, great tasting, and high in omega-3. Together with red peppers and garlic, this is an unbeatable combination.

3 red peppers, seeded and quartered
$^1/_2$ cup pine nuts, toasted
1 cup fresh bread crumbs
3 garlic cloves, finely chopped
Olive-oil spray (see page 17)
Freshly ground black pepper
4 'spatchcocked' trout (ask at your fishmarket for the trout to
   be opened and filleted, with the head and tail removed)

Serves 4

Char the peppers in the oven or broiler, or over a gas flame until the skin is blackened. Place the peppers in a paper bag and seal. Let the peppers steam in their own heat for 15 minutes, then remove and peel. Place in a food processor, along with their juice, and blend.

Add the pine nuts, bread crumbs, and garlic, and blend again to a smooth purée. With the food processor running, add the olive oil in a thin stream. Season with black pepper to taste.

Rub the trout on both sides with the red pepper purée. Refrigerate for 30 minutes.

Heat a ridged grill plate, large frying pan, or barbecue, until very hot. Lightly spray pan the surface with olive oil and cook the trout, flesh-side down, for three minutes. Turn the fish carefully and cook for a further three minutes.

Transfer to a serving platter and serve with noodles, rice, or new potatoes.

PER SERVING:
369 CALORIES, 16G FAT, 3G SATURATED FAT, 18G CARBOHYDRATE, 0.2G SODIUM

chile-corn crabcakes

Crabcakes are an all-time favorite of mine and these can be made the day before and stored in the fridge. White crabmeat comes from the claw, the brown meat from the body. Serve with a green salad.

1 pound white crabmeat, picked over
8 ounces brown crabmeat
1 chile, finely diced
1 onion, finely diced
$^1/_2$ red pepper, seeded and finely diced
2 celery stalks, finely diced
7 ounces canned corn, drained (about $^3/_4$ cup)
2 teaspoons chopped dill
$^2/_3$ cup plain yogurt
1 teaspoon mustard powder
2 eggs, lightly beaten
$1^1/_4$ cups fresh whole wheat bread crumbs
3 tablespoons rapeseed (canola) oil
Freshly ground black pepper

Serves 6

In a large bowl, mix together the white and brown crab meat, chile, onion, red pepper, celery, corn, and dill.

Combine the yogurt, mustard powder, and eggs in another bowl and then slowly add half the oil. Add the crab mixture and mix well. Fold in a third of the bread crumbs, or as much as you need to firm the mixture, and season to taste with black pepper. Refrigerate for two hours ideally.

Make the mixture into six large or 12 small patties. Coat each one in the remaining bread crumbs. These cakes can be made well ahead of when they are needed; at this point put them in the fridge to dry out overnight.

Heat the remaining oil in a large pan over medium heat, and cook the cakes for three minutes on each side. Serve hot.

PER SERVING:
306 CALORIES, 16G FAT, 3G SATURATED FAT, 14G CARBOHYDRATE, 0.64G SODIUM

chicken liver pâté

The easiest pâté I know, this takes just minutes to prepare. Eat hot or cold, with pickles, Melba toast, or crusty whole-grain bread, for a great snack or lunch.

Rapeseed (canola) oil spray (see page 17)
8 ounces chicken livers, cleaned (1 cup)
1 1/4 cups skim milk
3 egg yolks
1 shallot, finely diced
1 garlic clove, finely diced
1 teaspoon soft thyme leaves
Freshly ground black pepper
2/3 cup fresh bread crumbs

Serves 4

Preheat the oven to 325°F.

Lightly spray four small molds or ramekins with oil. Put the livers, milk, egg yolks, shallot, garlic, and thyme in a food processor and blend until smooth. Season with black pepper.

Put through a fine wire mesh strainer and then fold in the bread crumbs.

Spoon the mixture into the molds and then place in a roasting tray. Add hot water to the tray until it comes three-quarters of way up the sides of the molds. Cook in the oven until the pâté has set, this should take about 20 minutes.

PER SERVING:
150 CALORIES, 6G FAT, 2G SATURATED FAT, 9G CARBOHYDRATE, 0.14G SODIUM

chicken stir-fry with black beans

Chinese food offers lots of flavors, but very little fat. In fact, along with the Mediterranean diet, it is one we could learn a few tips from.

1 egg white
1 tablespoon cornstarch
2 skinless chicken breasts, cut into thin strips
1/2 tablespoon peanut oil
2 garlic cloves, finely chopped
1-inch fresh ginger root, peeled and grated
Pinch of dried red chile flakes
1 tablespoon Chinese black beans, finely chopped
1 carrot, sliced on the diagonal
1/2 red pepper, seeded and cut into diamonds
1/2 yellow pepper, seeded and cut into diamonds
1/2 cup chicken stock
1 tablespoon reduced-salt dark soy sauce
2 tablespoons rice wine vinegar
Pinch of sugar
3 ounces sugar-snap peas
4 scallions, sliced on the diagonal

Serves 2

Lightly beat the egg white in a non-metallic bowl with half the cornstarch. Add the chicken, cover with plastic wrap and chill for 30 minutes (this is called velveting).

Place one and a quarter cups water in a pan and bring to a boil. Stir the chicken, and lift it from the bowl using a slotted spoon. Remove the pan from the heat and add the chicken, stirring to prevent it from sticking together. Return to the heat and cook for one and a half minutes or until the chicken is white and just tender. Drain on paper towels.

Heat a wok and swirl in the oil. Add the garlic, ginger, chile flakes, and black beans, and stir-fry for 15 seconds, then add the carrot and stir-fry for one minute. Stir in the cooked chicken and the peppers. Pour in the stock, then add the soy sauce, vinegar, and sugar, stirring to combine. Increase the heat and bring to a boil, then reduce to a simmer. Add the sugar-snap peas and scallions and cook for two minutes. Mix the remaining cornstarch with one tablespoon water, and stir into the wok. Cook for a minute or so until the sauce clears and thickens.

Serve at once in Chinese-style bowls with steamed rice.

PER SERVING:
289 CALORIES, 5G FAT, 1G SATURATED FAT, 22G CARBOHYDRATE, 0.95G SODIUM

hot chile chicken fajitas

Mexico in its most popular foodie form. The cool flavors of the salsa take the edge off the hot chicken marinade, and it needs no further accompaniment. Cook on the barbecue or a grill pan.

1 tablespoon chile oil
1 tablespoon hot chile powder
1 tablespoon paprika
Pinch of sugar
Grated peel and juice of 1 lime
2 skinless chicken breast fillets
4 soft flour tortillas
$^1/_4$ small iceberg lettuce, shredded
$^2/_3$ cup low-fat yogurt

For the tomato and avocado salsa
2 large tomatoes, seeded and finely diced
1 red chile, seeded and finely chopped
Juice of 1 lime
$^1/_2$ small red onion, finely chopped
1 ripe avocado, peeled, pitted and finely diced
1 tablespoon olive oil
$^1/_2$ cup roughly chopped cilantro
Freshly ground black pepper

Serves 4

Soak eight six-inch bamboo skewers in water overnight.

Mix together the chile oil, chile powder, paprika, sugar, and the lime peel and juice in a shallow non-metallic dish.

Cut each chicken breast lengthwise into six strips. Add to the chile mixture and stir until well coated, then cover with plastic wrap and let marinate in the fridge for one to two hours.

To make the tomato and avocado salsa, place all the ingredients into a large bowl and stir gently to combine. Season with black pepper to taste and spoon into a serving bowl. Cover with plastic wrap and set aside to let the flavors

develop, but don't make this too far in advance, otherwise the avocado may blacken.

Heat a grill pan or a barbecue. Thread three pieces of chicken onto each soaked bamboo skewer, and place on the grill pan or barbecue. Cook for three to four minutes on each side or until the chicken is cooked through and lightly charred.

Heat a frying pan or grill pan. Add a tortilla and heat for 30 seconds, or until soft and pliable, turning once. Repeat with the remaining tortillas and stack up on a warmed plate. Place the chicken skewers on a serving platter and pass around the tomato and avocado salsa, warmed tortillas, lettuce, and yogurt, letting each person assemble the fajitas themselves.

PER SERVING:
392 CALORIES, 15G FAT, 2G SATURATED FAT, 42G CARBOHYDRATE, 0.27G SODIUM

souvlakia

Memories of Greek holidays, hot sun, white sands, and warm seas. This Mediterranean staple makes a simple but filling meal, great also for packed lunches and picnics.

8 ounces lamb fillets, cut into $1/2$-inch slices
$1/2$ onion, grated
3 garlic cloves, mashed to a paste with a little salt
1 teaspoon freshly ground black pepper
1 teaspoon ground cumin
$1/2$ teaspoon cayenne pepper
2 tablespoons olive oil
2 whole wheat pita breads
Juice of $1/2$ lemon
$1/4$ cup low-fat yogurt
$1/2$ teaspoon chopped fresh mint leaves
$1/2$ teaspoon chopped fresh cilantro
3 scallions, sliced

Serves 2

Toss the lamb with the onion, garlic, black pepper, cumin, cayenne pepper, and one tablespoon olive oil. Let marinate for as long as possible and at least an hour.

Heat the remaining olive oil in a heavy saucepan and cook the lamb for two minutes on each side. Warm the pita breads, and cut the edges to form a pocket. Stuff the lamb into the pocket and dribble with the lemon juice, yogurt, fresh herbs, and scallions.

PER SERVING:
478 CALORIES, 23G FAT, 7G SATURATED FAT, 38G CARBOHYDRATE, 0.5G SODIUM

linguine with fiery shrimp

Add a little fire to your belly. The tomato sauce has a surprising kick to it that will wake up your appetite and warm your mouth.

3 tablespoons olive oil
2 teaspoons dried red chile flakes or dried crushed chilees
1 teaspoon chopped thyme
One 14^1/$_2$-ounce can chopped tomatoes
5 garlic cloves, finely chopped
9 ounces baby spinach (about 2^1/$_2$-3^1/$_2$ cups)
Freshly ground black pepper
1 pound jumbo shrimp, shelled and split lengthwise
8 ounces dried whole wheat linguine
2 tablespoons chopped flat-leaf parsley

Serves 4

Heat half the oil in a frying-pan over medium heat. Add the chile flakes and cook for one minute. Add the thyme, tomatoes, and half the garlic, and stir well to combine. Cook for about 15 minutes, until the sauce has reduced and thickened. Fold in the spinach leaves and cook for three minutes. Season with black pepper to taste.

In a separate pan, heat the remaining oil with the remaining garlic. When the garlic begins to color, add the shrimp and cook until just pink, this should take about two minutes. Keep warm.

Meanwhile, cook the linguine in plenty of boiling water until al dente. Drain and place in a warm shallow serving dish. Add the shrimp, tomato sauce, and parsley to the linguine and combine thoroughly. Serve immediately.

PER SERVING:
385 CALORIES, 11G FAT, 2G SATURATED FAT, 43G CARBOHYDRATE, 0.47G SODIUM

fettuccine with purple sprouting broccoli

If you cannot find purple sprouting broccoli (a delicious springtime specialty), then substitute using regular broccoli, but be sure to peel any tough stems.

1 onion, finely diced
1 garlic clove, finely chopped
4 canned anchovy fillets, drained, rinsed and finely chopped
2 teaspoons canned capers, drained, rinsed, and chopped
1 teaspoon rosemary leaves
1 tablespoon chopped flat-leaf parsley
1 tablespoon olive oil
12 ounces purple sprouting broccoli (if unavailable, use regular broccoli with tough stems peeled), cut into
2-inch pieces (about 6 cups)
1 pound fresh fettuccine
Juice of ^{1}/$_2$ lemon
Freshly ground black pepper
Parmesan cheese shavings

Serves 4

In a saucepan, cook the first six ingredients in the olive oil, until the onions have softened without coloring.

Meanwhile, boil the broccoli in plenty of boiling water for two minutes, add the fettuccine, and cook for a further three minutes. When the pasta is cooked and the broccoli has broken up slightly, remove and drain.

Place the pasta and broccoli in a bowl and combine with the hot dressing. Add the lemon juice and season with black pepper to taste. Serve sprinkled with shavings of Parmesan.

PER SERVING:
387 CALORIES, 7G FAT, 1G SATURATED FAT, 68G CARBOHYDRATE, 0.22G SODIUM

green pasta

The herbs and spinach provide this pasta with a little extra goodness. Quick and simple, this is also low in fat, but immensely satisfying. Great for a light lunch or dinner.

12 ounces orsi or risoni
  (rice-shaped pasta)
2 tablespoons olive oil
2 garlic cloves, finely chopped
Pinch of dried chile flakes
2 handfuls of spinach, chopped
6 scallions, finely sliced
2 Bibb lettuces, shredded
Handful flat-leaf parsley leaves, roughly chopped
12 basil leaves, ripped
Juice of 1 lemon

Serves 6

Cook the pasta in a large pot of boiling water, then drain and return to the pot.

Meanwhile, heat the olive oil in a large wok, add the garlic and chile flakes, and cook for one minute. Add the spinach and, using a pair of tongs, keep turning the spinach over until it has wilted, this should take about three minutes. Add the remaining ingredients and cook for a further two minutes. Season with black pepper to taste.

Add the greens to the pasta and toss to combine, then serve immediately.

PER SERVING:
247 CALORIES, 5G FAT, 1G SATURATED FAT, 45G CARBOHYDRATE, 0.02G SODIUM

black olive dip

Another Mediterranean must, this is great served with raw vegetables or spread on whole-grain toast. A dip that will keep you coming back for more until you run out of vegetables.

8 ounces black olives, pitted
  (about 2½ cups)
2 tablespoons olive oil
2 garlic cloves, finely chopped
Pinch of dried red chile flakes
½ tsp ground black pepper
1 tablespoon tinned capers, drained
  and rinsed
Grated zest and juice of 1 lemon
1 tablespoon chopped parsley

Serves 8

Blend all the ingredients in a food processor and blitz until smooth – unless you prefer to leave it slightly chunky.

PER SERVING:
57 CALORIES, 6G FAT, 1G SATURATED FAT, 1G CARBOHYDRATE, 0.68G SODIUM

fiery marinated olives

12 ounces black and/or
  green olives, pitted, rinsed,
  and dried (about 2-2¼ cups)
1 teaspoon harissa or chile sauce
¼ cup lemon juice
1 heaped tablespoon pickled
  lemon rind, chopped (optional)
1 cup olive oil
Finely pared peel of 1 orange
  (unwaxed, if possible)
2 garlic cloves, quartered

Yield: 2½ cups

Place all the ingredients in a non-metallic bowl and stir until well combined. Transfer to a sterilized jar with a tight-fitting lid or simply leave in the bowl and cover tightly with plastic wrap. Set aside for four days or up to two weeks before eating (after that, the garlic could become rancid).

Drain the oil and lay the olives on paper towels to remove any excess oil before serving. Be warned – they are very potent.

PER 25G:
57 CALORIES, 6.2G FAT, 0.9G SATURATED FAT, 0G CARBOHYDRATE, 0.49G SODIUM

4

main courses

saffron pea pilaf

A pilaf is a Middle Eastern rice dish, often cooked with meat or vegetables. In a pilaf, the grains of rice should remain as separate as possible, so the rice is first rinsed thoroughly.

1¹/₃ cups brown rice
1 tablespoon olive oil
2 tablespoons margarine
3 tablespoons slivered almonds
8 walnut halves, roughly chopped
2 tablespoons raisins
8 dried apricots, diced
4 cloves
2 cardamom pods
1-inch cinnamon stick

¹/₂ teaspoon saffron strands, soaked in a little warm water
4 scallions, thinly sliced
Freshly ground black pepper
4 cups vegetable or chicken stock
13 ounces shelled peas (about 3-3¹/₂ cups) – fresh or frozen
3 tablespoons chopped cilantro

Serves 4

Rinse the rice with cold water, then drain and set aside. Heat the olive oil and margarine in a large heavy pan that has a tight-fitting lid. Add the almonds, walnuts, raisins, and apricots, and cook for about five minutes, until the nuts are golden brown and the raisins are plumped up, stirring occasionally and taking care that nothing burns. Remove the fruit and nuts with a slotted spoon and set aside.

Add the cloves, cardamom pods, and cinnamon stick to the pan. Cook gently for a minute or two until they become aromatic, stirring continuously. Add the drained rice to the pan and cook for two minutes, stirring to ensure all the rice grains are coated, then stir in the saffron mixture, the scallions and a half-teaspoon pepper. Pour in the stock, bring to a boil, then reduce the heat, cover, and simmer for 45 minutes or until the rice is fluffed up and completely tender. Add more stock as necessary, but remember it should end up quite dry.

When the pilaf has nearly finished cooking, place the peas in a pan of boiling water and simmer for two to three minutes until tender, then drain. Remove the pilaf from the heat and add the peas, fruit, and nut mixture, and the cilantro. Gently fold in, using a large metal spoon, until well combined. Season with black pepper to taste and serve hot.

PER SERVING:
492 CALORIES, 19G FAT, 3G SATURATED FAT, 70G CARBOHYDRATE, 0.38G SODIUM

pumpkin risotto with leek and yogurt

Risottos are usually quite high in fat since they are generally made with cream, butter, and cheese. This version uses less cheese and lowfat yogurt.

2 tablespoons olive oil
12 ounces pumpkin, peeled and cut into 1-inch dice (about 3 cups)
2 leeks, sliced
1 tablespoon chopped sage
Freshly ground black pepper
2 onions, finely chopped
1 heaped teaspoon fresh thyme leaves

1 fresh bay leaf
1¹/₃ cups arborio (risotto) rice
One 4-ounce glass dry white wine
4 cups vegetable stock, boiling
¹/₂ cup grated Parmesan cheese
¹/₃ cup plain yogurt
2 tablespoons flat-leaf parsley, chopped

Serves 4

Heat half of the oil in a large sauté pan, add the pumpkin, and cook over a fairly high heat for about five minutes, until lightly caramelized, tossing occasionally. Reduce the heat, add the leeks and sage, and cook over gentle heat, stirring occasionally, for another two to three minutes, until softened but not colored, and the pumpkin is completely tender when pierced with the tip of a sharp knife. Season with black pepper, tip into a bowl, and set aside.

Add the remaining oil to the pumpkin pan, then tip in the onions, thyme, and bay leaf, and cook for a few minutes until softened but not colored, stirring occasionally.

Add the rice to the onion mixture and continue to cook for another minute, stirring to ensure that all the grains are well coated. Pour in the wine and let it bubble down, stirring until it is completely absorbed.

Begin to add the boiling stock a ladle at a time, stirring frequently. Let each ladleful be almost completely absorbed before adding the next. After approximately 20 minutes, add the pumpkin mixture, the Parmesan, yogurt, and parsley, and stir energetically to combine.

Season with black pepper to taste, and serve immediately with a big bowl of salad greens.

PER SERVING:
359 CALORIES, 10G FAT, 3G SATURATED FAT, 54G CARBOHYDRATE, 0.41G SODIUM

smoked haddock and potato "risotto"

Smoked food tends to be high in salt, so keep the rest of your day's salt intake as low as possible. Children, pregnant women, and the elderly should not eat undercooked eggs.

2¹/₂ cups lowfat milk
1 onion, cut in half
1 fresh bay leaf
8 ounces undyed smoked haddock
1 garlic clove, finely chopped
2 scallions, finely sliced
1 sprig thyme

1 tablespoon olive oil
8 ounces unpeeled new
  potatoes, diced
  (about 1¹/₂ cups)
¹/₂ cup grated Parmesan
  cheese
2 tablespoons plain yogurt
Freshly ground black pepper
2 soft poached eggs

Serves 2

Heat the milk in a saucepan along with the onion and bay leaf. Remove from the heat and let infuse for 15 minutes. Return to the heat. When simmering, add the fish and cook for eight minutes. Remove the fish and set aside, then strain the cooking liquid and set that aside.

Cook the garlic, scallions, and thyme in the olive oil for five minutes, then add the potatoes and cooking milk, and cook until the potatoes are tender, this should take about 12 minutes.

Flake the smoked haddock, discarding any skin or bones, and fold into the potato mix. Fold in the Parmesan and yogurt, then season with black pepper to taste.

Fill a pot with water and bring to a boil, the water should be at least four and a half inches deep. Add one and a half tablespoons vinegar for every quart of water. Crack each egg into a cup and slide the egg into the water at the exact point where it has a rolling boil. After two to three minutes of cooking, lift the eggs with a slotted spoon and lower them into iced water.

Warm through the poached eggs and place one on each warm plate. Top with the smoked haddock "risotto."

PER SERVING:
506 CALORIES, 22G FAT, 9G SATURATED FAT, 35G CARBOHYDRATE, 1.25G SODIUM

shrimp and saffron risotto

A more traditional risotto than the smoked haddock and potato version (left), this is a creamy emulsion of flavor and texture, rich and very delicious.

5 cups fish stock
3 tablespoons olive oil
1 onion, finely diced
3 garlic cloves, finely diced
2 red chiles, finely diced
¹/₂ teaspoon chopped thyme
2 fresh bay leaves

2 cups Arborio (risotto) rice
2 tablespoons dry vermouth
2 pinches of saffron strands, soaked
  in 2 tablespoons cold water
36 raw, shelled shrimp
20 basil leaves, torn
2 tablespoons pesto
2 tablespoons plain yogurt
Freshly ground black pepper

Serves 4

Bring the fish stock to a boil in a large pot and keep to a simmer.

Heat another large saucepan or pot and add the olive oil. Stir in the onion, garlic, chiles, thyme, and bay leaves, and cook until the onion is soft but without color. Add the rice and cook for three minutes.

Add the vermouth and stir until the liquid is almost completely absorbed. Add the saffron, along with its soaking liquid and a ladle of hot fish stock. Before adding more stock, let the rice absorb the liquid. Stir the rice frequently. Continue to add hot stock, a ladleful at a time, making sure each addition is absorbed before adding the next. The idea is to keep the rice creamy and thick like a sauce. As you add more stock, the rice will release its starches and start to puff up. After about 20 minutes, nibble on a grain of rice to see whether it is cooked; there should still be a little bite to it.

When the risotto is ready, it will have a creamy texture, with the grains of rice still separate. Add the shrimp and basil, stirring as you cook for an additional two minutes. Fold in the pesto, yogurt, and seasoning. Serve immediately, with a green salad.

PER SERVING:
531 CALORIES, 12G FAT, 2G SATURATED FAT, 78G CARBOHYDRATE, 0.64G SODIUM

bay-scented salmon on roasted vegetables

Salmon is fantastic fish, full of omega-3 fats, but farmed salmon can be less flavorful than wild. Either way, this dish provides all the taste it needs.

3 small carrots, cut in half
2 small parsnips, cut in half
6 large shallots
1/2 small butternut squash, peeled, seeded, and cut into wedges
2 garlic cloves, crushed
1 red chile, seeded and finely chopped

1 teaspoon fresh thyme leaves
1 tablespoon olive oil
1 teaspoon freshly ground black pepper
Olive-oil spray (see page 17)
16 fresh bay leaves
4 x 6-ounce salmon steaks
Juice and peel of 1 lime
3 tablespoons chopped chervil

Serves 4

Place half the bay leaves on a plate, top with the salmon steaks and the remaining bay leaves, and season with ground black pepper. Cover with plastic wrap and refrigerate for one hour.

Preheat the oven to 375°F. Place the carrots, parsnips, whole shallots, and the squash in a pan of boiling water and blanch for two to three minutes, then refresh under cold running water to retain their color. Toss together the cooked vegetables, garlic, chile, and thyme, along with the olive oil, and place in a preheated baking dish. Pop in the oven and roast for 45 minutes or until the vegetables are tender and golden, turning from time to time. Season with black pepper to taste.

About 10 minutes before the vegetables are ready, lightly spray a baking tray with olive oil. Place the bay leaves and the salmon on top, spray the salmon with a little oil, and season with black pepper. Broil for five minutes on each side.

Serve the salmon on a bed of the roasted vegetables, squeeze a little lime juice over the salmon, sprinkle with the lime peel and chervil, and serve with lime wedges.

PER SERVING:
422 CALORIES, 23G FAT, 4G SATURATED FAT, 17G CARBOHYDRATE, 0.1G SODIUM

salmon with pea and watercress purée

Steaming is one of the best ways to cook, since the food retains more nutrients, but it is perceived as boring. This should change your mind. Most of the fat here is unsaturated.

Olive-oil spray (see page 17)
4 scallions, thinly sliced
1 1/2 cups shelled peas (fresh or frozen)
1 1/4 cups vegetable stock
3 ounces watercress (about 1–1 1/2 cups)
2 tablespoons plain yogurt
Freshly ground black pepper
2 x 6-ounce salmon steaks
Lemon wedges
Steamed new potatoes, for serving

Serves 2

Heat a non-stick sauté pan and lightly spray with oil. Add the scallions and cook for a few minutes until softened, stirring occasionally. Add the peas and stock to the pan, stirring to combine. Cover with a circle of wax paper and let sweat for two to three minutes.

Remove the paper and add the watercress, reserving a little for the garnish, then let cook for a further two minutes or until all the liquid has evaporated. Place in a food processor along with the yogurt, and blend until nearly smooth – you still want a little texture. Season with black pepper to taste. Set aside.

Season the salmon fillets with black pepper and steam for six minutes; alternatively, wrap them in foil and place in a preheated oven at 400°F for eight minutes.

Place the salmon on the pea purée and top with the lemon wedges and reserved watercress. Serve with new potatoes.

PER SERVING:
431 CALORIES, 23G FAT, 5G SATURATED FAT, 13G CARBOHYDRATE, 0.31G SODIUM

baked cod with olives and scallions

A different way of cooking white fish. Cod is a great fish because it absorbs flavors so easily. This is a flavorful recipe, reminiscent again of the Mediterranean.

1 teaspoon olive oil
2 x 6-ounce cod fillets
16 black olives, pitted and finely chopped
2 tablespoons chopped parsley
1 tablespoon chopped dill
1 bunch scallions, finely chopped
2 chiles, finely diced
Juice and peel of 1 lime
Freshly ground black pepper
$^2/_3$ cup tomato juice
$^2/_3$ cup fish stock

Serves 2

Preheat the oven to 450°F.

Lightly oil a flameproof roasting tray or other flameproof and ovenproof plan, and place the cod in the bottom. In a bowl, combine the olives, herbs, scallons, chiles, and lime peel with the lime juice, then spread this mixture over the top of the cod.

Season with black pepper, then pour the tomato juice and fish stock around the fish. Place on the burner and bring to a boil over medium heat.

Place the dish in the oven and cook for 12 minutes. Serve immediately, using the juices as a sauce, with an herb leaf salad.

PER SERVING:
209 CALORIES, 6G FAT, 1G SATURATED FAT, 5G CARBOHYDRATE, 0.92G SODIUM

roast cod with anchovy and garlic

Another oven-cooked cod dish, but with a completely different taste. Anchovies are one of my favorite flavorings and give this recipe a completely new dimension.

5 canned anchovy fillets, drained, rinsed, and roughly chopped
2 teaspoons finely chopped mint
8 garlic cloves, finely chopped
4 x 7-ounce cod steaks
3 tablespoons seasoned all-purpose flour
2 tablespoons rapeseed (canola) oil
4 shallots, halved
2 celery stalks, finely sliced
1 carrot, finely sliced
2 tablespoons dry vermouth
One 14$^1/_2$-ounce can chopped tomatoes
2 cups fish stock
3 tablespoons chopped flat-leaf parsley
Freshly ground black pepper

Serves 4

Preheat the oven to 400°F. Soak the anchovies in cold water for 30 minutes. Drain, then, in a food processor, blend the anchovies, with the mint and half the garlic, to a smooth paste.

Make four one-inch incisions in each of the cod steaks and push the paste into the slits. Dust the cod all over with seasoned flour.

Heat the oil in a flameproof casserole dish or other flameproof and ovenproof pan. Brown the cod steaks all over, then remove and set aside.

Add the shallots, celery, carrot, and remaining garlic to the same casserole dish, and cook until the vegetables start to soften. Return the cod to the pan and add the vermouth, tomatoes, and fish stock, and bring to a boil. Remove from the burner and place in the oven. Bake for 15 minutes, then fold in the parsley.

Season with black pepper to taste and serve in deep bowls, with brown rice or new potatoes.

PER SERVING:
308 CALORIES, 8G FAT, 1G SATURATED FAT, 16G CARBOHYDRATE, 0.51G SODIUM

teriyaki tuna with roast garlic noodles

Tuna lends itself to punchy flavors and this Japanese-style dish provides plenty of them. Teriyaki is a sweet-tasting sauce used to broil chicken, beef, and fish.

3 tablespoons reduced-salt light
   soy sauce
3 tablespoons mirin or dry sherry
1 tablespoons soft brown sugar
1 tablespoon grated fresh ginger root
1 bulb garlic plus 2 garlic cloves

4 tuna steaks, about
   1-inch thick
2 tablespoons olive oil
4 scallions, finely chopped
1 teaspoon chopped thyme
10 ounces dried egg noodles
3 ounces baby spinach leaves
   (about 1½ large handfuls)
Freshly ground black pepper

Serves 4

Preheat the oven to 375°F. In a shallow dish, combine the soy sauce, mirin or dry sherry, sugar, and ginger. Finely chop the two garlic cloves and add to the dish. Add the tuna and cover. Refrigerate for two hours, turning from time to time.

Cut a quarter-inch from the top of the garlic bulb, revealing the cut edges of the garlic cloves. Drizzle with a teaspoon of the olive oil, wrap in foil, and roast in the oven for about 30 minutes, or until the garlic is soft, then let cool slightly.

Squeeze the softened garlic from each clove into a frying pan, add the remaining oil, the scallions, and thyme, and cook over moderate heat until the onions are softened but not colored.

Cook the noodles in boiling water, according to the package instructions. Drain and tip into the garlic and onion mixture, toss to combine, and fold in the spinach leaves. Toss until the spinach has wilted, and season with black pepper to taste.

Preheat the broiler. Cook the tuna for two minutes on each side, depending on how rare you like your fish, basting with the marinade several times during cooking. Serve immediately on the noodles.

PER SERVING:
573 CALORIES, 18G FAT, 4G SATURATED FAT, 57G CARBOHYDRATE, 0.71G SODIUM

spicy fish curry

We don't eat enough fish curries and I can never understand why. This dish has beautifully balanced flavors and, unlike most curries, is relatively low in fat.

1½ pounds fish fillets (salmon, cod, or monkfish)
Olive-oil spray (see page 17)
2 onions, thinly sliced
6 garlic cloves, finely diced
½ teaspoon ground coriander
½ teaspoon ground turmeric
1 teaspoon cayenne pepper
½ teaspoon ground ginger
3 tomatoes, seeded and chopped
8 ounces leaf spinach, stems removed (about 2-3 cups)
Freshly ground black pepper
⅔ cup plain yogurt

Serves 4

Cut the fish into 1-inch cubes.

Lightly spray a non-stick frying pan with olive oil, add the fish, and fry until just cooked, this should take about three minutes. Remove and set aside.

Spray a little more oil into the pan and fry the onions until they are soft but not colored, then add the garlic and spices and cook for a further five minutes. Add the tomatoes and spinach and cook until the spinach has wilted. Season with black pepper, then add the yogurt. Bring to a boil and simmer for five minutes.

Return the fish to the sauce and heat through. Serve immediately with brown rice.

PER SERVING:
328 CALORIES, 14G FAT, 3G SATURATED FAT, 12G CARBOHYDRATE, 0.21G SODIUM

spiced fish casserole

Simple one-pot dining, inspired by the West Indies. Allspice is mainly cultivated in Jamaica and is so called because it tastes like a combination of cloves, pepper, nutmeg, and cinnamon.

$^1/_2$ teaspoon freshly ground black pepper
8 allspice berries, crushed
4 garlic cloves, crushed
2 hot chiles, finely chopped
Juice of 2 limes
1 tablespoon olive oil
4 ounces monkfish
4 ounces haddock
4 raw jumbo shrimp, shelled
4 large diver-caught scallops, shucked
$2^1/_2$ cups fish stock
3 ounces green beans, cut into 1-inch pieces
$^1/_3$ cup corn niblets
$^1/_2$ cup shelled peas (fresh or frozen)
4 scallions
Lime wedges, for serving

Serves 4

Combine the first six ingredients in a bowl to make a marinade. Place all the fish and shellfish in the marinade for one hour.

When ready to cook, add the fish and the shellfish along with the marinade to the stock and bring to a rolling boil.

Add all the vegetables and cook for four minutes.

Serve the fish in bowls, covering the fish with the cooking liquid, accompanied by lime wedges and crusty bread.

PER SERVING:
153 CALORIES, 4G FAT, 1G SATURATED FAT, 8G CARBOHYDRATE, 0.36G SODIUM

moroccan-spiced roast mackerel

Mackerel has the wonderful ability to carry big flavors. It is also one of the richest sources of omega-3 fats, hence the fat content of this dish.

2 tablespoons rapeseed (canola) or olive oil
2 tablespoons chopped cilantro
1 teaspoon chopped mint leaves
Juice of 1 lemon
$1/2$ teaspoon chile powder
$1/2$ teaspoon paprika
2 teaspoons ground cumin
1 teaspoon ground coriander
4 garlic cloves, crushed
$1/2$ teaspoon freshly ground black pepper
4 x 12-ounce whole mackerel, filleted
$1/4$ cup plain yogurt

Serves 4

In a bowl, mix together the oil, chopped cilantro, mint, lemon juice, chili powder, paprika, cumin, ground coriander, garlic, and black pepper.

Place the mackerel fillets in the marinade and coat all over.

Marinate for 30 minutes, turning from time to time.

Preheat the oven to 375°F.

Place the fish and the marinade in a shallow flameproof baking dish or other flameproof or ovenproof pan, add a half-cup water and bring to a boil. Transfer to the oven and roast for 12–15 minutes. Remove from the oven and keep warm.

Strain the cooking juices into a saucepan and fold in the yogurt. Warm through, season with black pepper, and pour over the mackerel.

PER SERVING:
633 CALORIES, 47G FAT, 8G SATURATED FAT, 4G CARBOHYDRATE, 0.18G SODIUM

oatmeal herrings with peppers and anchovies

Most of us only try herrings as kippers, when they have been cold-smoked, but they are best when fresh. Accompany with lower-salt dishes.

4 x 13-ounce herrings, cleaned
2 slices lean Canadian bacon
$1^{1}/4$ cups skim milk
$1^{1}/3$ cups coarse oatmeal
Olive-oil spray (see page 17)
1 large onion, finely sliced
3 garlic cloves, finely chopped
3 tablespoons dry vermouth
One $10^{1}/2$-ounce jar roasted red peppers and sun-dried tomatoes, drained and dried on paper towels
$1^{1}/2$ pounds plum tomatoes, peeled and chopped (about $3^{1}/2$-4 cups)
1 teaspoon chopped marjoram leaves
1 teaspoon chopped canned capers
2 canned anchovy fillets, drained, rinsed, and chopped
16 black olives, pitted and cut in half

Serves 4

Preheat the oven to 400°F.

Make two diagonal slashes in each side of each herring. Cut each slice of bacon into eight pieces and insert into the slashes in the herrings. Dip the herrings in the milk, and then smother all over with the oatmeal.

Lightly spray a frying pan with olive oil, and heat it. Add the onion and garlic and cook until the onion is softened but not colored. Add the vermouth, red peppers and sun-dried tomatoes, plum tomatoes, marjoram, capers, anchovies, and olives. Simmer for 10 minutes. Tip this mixture into a baking dish, big enough to accommodate the four herrings.

In the same frying pan, spray with a little more olive oil and pan-fry the herrings for one minute on each side. Remove the herrings and place on the pepper mix and bake for 20 minutes.

Serve with new potatoes or a green salad.

PER SERVING:
754 CALORIES, 44G FAT, 6G SATURATED FAT, 44G CARBOHYDRATE, 1.34G SODIUM

bouillabaisse

Entertaining in style, here are some great flavors. This is another fantastic Mediterranean recipe that traditionally contains several kinds of rock fish, saffron, onions, garlic, and tomatoes.

2 tablespoons olive oil
2 onions, finely chopped
4 garlic cloves, finely chopped
2 leeks, trimmed and finely chopped
1 fennel head, finely chopped, fronds reserved
One 14^1/$_2$-ounce can chopped tomatoes
1 teaspoon fennel seeds
1 tablespoon tomato paste
1 small bunch flat-leaf parsley, separated into leaves and stalks
2 sprigs of thyme
2 bay leaves
1 pound fish bones (optional)
2 strips pared orange peel
2^1/$_2$ cups fish stock
2^1/$_4$ cups spring water
1/2 teaspoon saffron strands, soaked in a little warm water
4 medium floury potatoes, peeled and cut in half
1 tablespoon Pernod
Freshly ground black pepper
1 red mullet, scaled and filleted, each fillet cut in half, head and bones reserved
2 x 4^1/$_2$-ounce sea bass fillets, cut in half
8 ounce monkfish fillet, cut into 1^1/$_2$-inch chunks
1 pound mussels, cleaned (about 20 in total)
6 raw large tiger shrimp, shelled and de-veined, shells reserved

Serves 4

Heat the olive oil in a large pot. Add the onions, garlic, leeks, and fennel, and cook gently for 10 minutes or until the vegetables are soft, but not colored, stirring occasionally. Stir in the tomatoes, fennel seeds, tomato paste, parsley stalks, thyme, and bay leaves, then add the reserved bones, if using, and the fish trimmings and shrimp shells, stirring to coat. Cook for a minute or so, stirring until everything is well combined, then add the orange peel and pour in the fish stock, spring water, and saffron mixture. Bring to a boil, then reduce the heat and simmer gently, uncovered, for 30 minutes, skimming the surface occasionally to remove any froth. Strain and return to the pot, discarding the bones and shells.

Add the potatoes to the fish broth and cook for 15 minutes. Add the Pernod and season to taste with black pepper. Return to a simmer, then add the red mullet and the sea bass fillets along with the monkfish and mussels. Bring back up to a simmer and add the shrimp. Cover, and cook for another two minutes or until the mussels have opened and the shrimp have turned pink. Using a slotted spoon, transfer the fish and shellfish to a warm serving platter and pour the broth over them. Roughly chop the parsley leaves and scatter on top for serving.

PER SERVING:
447 CALORIES, 12G FAT, 2G SATURATED FAT, 35G CARBOHYDRATE, 0.58G SODIUM

chicken tagine

Most people associate spicy with hot, but not so in this full-flavored dish from Morocco. Made with either chicken or lamb, this stew is traditionally cooked over an open fire.

$^1/_2$ tablespoon ground ginger
1 teaspoon freshly ground
   black pepper
$^1/_2$ teaspoon ground cinnamon
$^1/_2$ teaspoons ground turmeric
2 teaspoons paprika
$^1/_2$ teaspoon cayenne pepper
8 boneless, skinless chicken thighs,
   cut into 1-inch pieces
1 tablespoon olive oil
6 garlic cloves, crushed to a paste
2 onions, grated

$^1/_3$ cup dried apricots, soaked
   in a little water
$^1/_4$ cup slivered almonds
2 tablespoons raisins or
   golden raisins
1 teaspoon honey
$^1/_2$ teaspoon saffron strands,
   soaked in a little cold water
1$^1/_4$ cups tomato juice
1$^1/_4$ cups chicken stock
One 14$^1/_2$-ounce can
   chopped tomatoes
2 tablespoons chopped cilantro

Serves 4

Mix all the spices together. Coat the chicken with half the spice mixture and leave overnight preferably, or for a minimum of two hours.

In a heavy saucepan, heat the oil and brown the chicken over a high heat. Remove from the pan and set aside. Add the remaining spice mixture, the crushed garlic, and grated onions to the pan. Let the onions soften without browning.

Add the apricots and their soaking water, the almonds, raisins, honey, saffron and its liquid, tomato juice, chicken stock, and tomatoes. Bring to a boil, reduce the heat to medium, and cook until the sauce has thickened considerably, this should take about 20 minutes. Add the chicken and cook for an additional 20 minutes.

Fold in the chopped cilantro and serve immediately with the Jeweled Couscous (see page 61).

PER SERVING:
356 CALORIES, 9G FAT, 1G SATURATED FAT, 26G CARBOHYDRATE, 0.42G SODIUM

chicken kabob tonnato

This is a fantastic broiled variation of a classic Italian veal dish, *Vitello tonnato*, which is also made with tuna and anchovies. Great for summer lunches.

$^1/_2$ onion, finely diced
$^1/_2$ carrot, finely diced
$^1/_2$ celery stalk, finely diced
2 garlic cloves, finely diced
$^1/_2$ teaspoon soft thyme leaves
1 bay leaf
2 tablespoons olive oil
4 ounces canned tuna in brine, drained (about 1/2 cup)
4 canned anchovy fillets
$^2/_3$ cup dry white wine
$^2/_3$ cup chicken stock
1$^1/_4$ cups lowfat yogurt
Pinch of salt
Freshly ground black pepper
2 x 6-ounce skinless chicken breast, cut into $^3/_4$-inch dice
Olive-oil spray (see page 17)

Serves 2

Cook the onion, carrot, celery, garlic, thyme, and bay leaf in the oil until the onion is soft but not brown. Add the tuna, anchovies, white wine, and stock, and simmer for 20 minutes or until a half-cup of liquid remains. Remove the bay leaf and blend the mixture in a food processor until smooth.

Let cool, then fold in the yogurt. Season with black pepper to taste.

Thread the chicken onto four satay or toothpicks, spray lightly with oil, and broil for three minutes on each side. Season with a little salt and black pepper. Serve the hot kabobs with the cold tuna sauce.

PER SERVING:
501 CALORIES, 16G FAT, 3G SATURATED FAT, 15G CARBOHYDRATE, 0.94G SODIUM

the "really useful chicken" recipe

This is exactly what it says it is: a really healthy way of cooking chicken that is delicious on its own or used in salads (see Asian chicken salad, page 73), sandwiches, or stew.

3¼ pounds free-range chicken, skin removed
4 scallions, sliced
3 x ¼-inch slices discs fresh ginger root
6 garlic cloves, peeled
1 chile
10 black peppercorns

Serves 4

Place the chicken in a pot, one that has a tightly fitting lid, cover with water, and add the remaining ingredients.

Bring to a boil and simmer for 35 minutes, turning the chicken once during the cooking process. Cover with a lid and turn off the heat. Let the chicken relax in the liquid for one hour.

Remove the chicken. Let cool completely, then cut up and use as needed.

PER SERVING:
212 CALORIES, 8G FAT, 3G SATURATED FAT, 0G CARBOHYDRATE, 0.09G SODIUM

broiled chicken with cilantro chutney

A very simple meal, quick to make and with lots of taste. Whenever possible, buy organic chicken as the flavor is noticeably better.

Olive-oil spray (see page 17)
2 x 6-ounce skinless chicken breasts
1 cup basmati rice, cooked

For the chutney
2 handfuls mint leaves
2 handfuls cilantro
1 small onion, roughly chopped
½-inch piece fresh ginger root, peeled and grated
1 chile, roughly chopped
½ teaspoon cumin seeds
1 garlic clove
2 teaspoons lemon juice
1 tablespoon dry unsweetened coconut, moistened in a little water

Serves 2

To make the chutney, blend the ingredients in a food processor until smooth.

Lightly spray the chicken breasts with oil and cook under a hot broiler for eight minutes on each side. Serve the chicken with the chutney, basmati rice, and a green salad.

PER SERVING:
546 CALORIES, 7G FAT, 4G SATURATED FAT, 75G CARBOHYDRATE, 0.12G SODIUM

tea-smoked quail

Home-smoking at its easiest: the tea, sugar, and rice make a simple smoking mixture, while the Asian marinade gives fantastic flavor. It also contains less salt than store-bought smoked food.

1 tablespoon sesame oil
2 tablespoons honey
1 tablespoon reduced-salt soy sauce
4 quail
2 tablespoons jasmine tea leaves
2 tablespoons raw sugar
2 tablespoons rice

Serves 2 (4 as a starter)

Combine the sesame oil, honey, and soy sauce in a bowl, rub it over the quail, and let the quail marinate in it for one hour.

Make a smoking mixture by combining the tea leaves, sugar, and rice. Cut a circle of foil that will fit the bottom of a wok, and scrunch the sides until you have made a container about four and a half inches in diameter. Place it in the bottom of the wok and put the smoking mixture in it.

Place the wok over the highest heat and, once the mixture starts to smoke, place the quail on a circular metal rack that fits halfway up the wok. Cover with a tight-fitting lid, and let it smoke for five minutes.

Remove the wok from the heat and let the quail continue to smoke without lifting the lid for one to two minutes.

Serve with Asian slaw (see page 73).

PER SERVING:
461 CALORIES, 29G FAT, 7G SATURATED FAT, 4G CARBOHYDRATE, 0.22G SODIUM

asian pork in lettuce leaves

A lovely way of serving and eating pork. The light Asian flavors and the fresh crunch of the lettuce leaves make this a delicious meal, hot or cold.

2 garlic cloves, finely chopped
1/2 heaped teaspoon freshly
   ground black pepper
Juice and peel of 1 lime
2 tablespoons chopped cilantro
1 tablespoon peanut or sunflower oil
8 ounces lean ground pork (1 cup)
1 tablespoon chopped
   unsalted peanuts
2 tablespoons chopped canned
bamboo shoots
1 tablespoon nam pla
   (Thai fish sauce) or
   reduced-salt light soy sauce
1 teaspoon honey
1 bird's eye chile, finely chopped
2 shallots, thinly sliced
2 large oranges, segmented
2 tablespoons chopped mint
2 Bibb lettuces, separated
   into leaves

Serves 2

Heat a large frying pan or wok. Mix together the garlic, pepper, lime juice and peel, and half of the cilantro in a small bowl. Add the oil to the pan, tip in the garlic mixture, and stir-fry for 30 seconds, then add the pork and stir-fry for 8–10 minutes until well browned, breaking up the ground pork with a wooden spoon as it cooks.

Add the peanuts, bamboo shoots, fish sauce or soy sauce, honey, and chile to the pork mixture and cook for another five minutes or until the liquid has almost completely evaporated, stirring occasionally. Season to taste.

Place the shallots in a bowl along with the orange segments and a heaped teaspoon each of the mint and remaining cilantro. Mix until well combined and pile into the middle of a large plate or platter. Stir the remaining mint and cilantro into the pork mixture and use to fill the lettuce leaves, arranging them around the orange salad.

Place a little of the orange salad on top of each pork wrap and eat immediately.

PER SERVING:
336 CALORIES, 14G FAT, 3G SATURATED FAT, 23G CARBOHYDRATE, 0.62G SODIUM

rice bake with pancetta, greens, and pecans

A really substantial meal, especially as most of the fat is unsaturated. This rice bake is great served with a green salad.

6 cups chicken stock
1 bay leaf
1 sprig thyme
1^1/$_3$ cups brown rice
2 tablespoons margarine
4 ounces pancetta or lean smoked bacon, roughly chopped
  (about 1 cup)
2 onions, finely chopped
3 celery stalks, finely chopped
^{1}/$_2$ Savoy cabbage, chopped
3 tablespoons finely chopped marjoram
^{1}/$_2$ sachet sage and onion stuffing
1 cup chopped pecans
Freshly ground black pepper
2 eggs, beaten
Olive-oil spray (see page 17)

Serves 6

Bring four cups of the stock, the bay leaf, and thyme to a boil. Add the rice, reduce the heat, cover, and cook for 30 minutes. Transfer the rice to a large bowl, discarding the bay leaf and thyme.

Meanwhile, melt the margarine in a large saucepan, add the pancetta or bacon, onions, and celery. Cook over medium heat for eight minutes until the onions are soft but not brown. Add the cabbage and marjoram and cook for five minutes, stirring regularly. Add this mixture to the rice, fold in the stuffing, pecans, plenty of black pepper, and the beaten eggs.

Lightly oil a large baking dish. Fold the remaining chicken stock into the stuffing and place in the baking dish. Cover with oiled foil and bake in a hot oven for 30 minutes.

PER SERVING:
425 CALORIES, 25G FAT, 4G SATURATED FAT, 39G CARBOHYDRATE, 0.69G SODIUM

ham bollito with salsa verde

Bollito misto usually contains several meats (it means "boiled mixed" in Italian), but this ham version is equally delicious. It is traditionally served with salsa verde.

4 small carrots, peeled and left whole
4 small onions, peeled, with root intact
3^1/$_4$ pound ham, soaked overnight in water and drained
2 celery hearts, quartered through the root end
12 black peppercorns
3 fresh bay leaves
Pared rind of 1 orange, studded with 4 whole cloves
12 parsley stalks
12 new salad potatoes, unpeeled
^{3}/$_4$ cup shelled fava beans (fresh or frozen)
12 baby leeks, trimmed
Salsa Verde (see page 62), for serving

Serves 8

Put the carrots and onions into a pot large enough to hug the ham and place the ham on top. Add the celery, peppercorns, bay leaves, and studded orange rind, then add enough water so that the liquid covers the ham completely.

Add the parsley stalks to a pan and bring to a boil. Reduce the heat and simmer for one hour, skimming off any scum that rises to the top and topping up with boiling water as needed to keep the ham completely covered. Cook the ham following the instructions on the wrapping – about 20 minutes per pound. Add the new potatoes 20 minutes before the end of the cooking time. Add the fava beans and leeks 10 minutes before the end. Discard the orange and parsley stalks.

Remove the ham from the pot, and place on a carving board. Snip away the string and cut away any excess fat, then carve into thick slices. Arrange the ham slices on serving plates and spoon a selection of the vegetables and a little broth around them. Serve with Salsa Verde and Dijon mustard.

PER SERVING:
267 CALORIES, 7G FAT, 2G SATURATED FAT, 12G CARBOHYDRATE, 1.39G SODIUM

tuscan-style lamb

Here are more wonderful flavors from Italy. This is a nutritious dish filled with the Mediterranean staples – tomatoes, beans, fish, olive oil, and garlic.

2 lamb sirloin chops, fat and
  skin removed
9 small sprigs of rosemary
4 garlic cloves, finely chopped
Freshly ground black pepper
Olive-oil spray (see page 17)
1 onion, finely chopped
2 carrots, diced
2 celery stalks, diced
1 heaped teaspoon fresh
  thyme leaves

4 canned anchovy fillets, rinsed,
  drained, and finely chopped
½ cup red wine
1¼ cups lamb or chicken stock
One 14½-ounce can chopped
  tomatoes
1 tablespoon tomato paste
One 15-ounce can cannellini
  beans, drained and rinsed
2 tablespoons chopped flat-leaf
  parsley

Serves 2

Toss the lamb chops with the rosemary and half the garlic and season with black pepper. Place in a non-metallic dish. Cover with plastic wrap and leave for an hour at room temperature or up to 24 hours in a fridge.

Heat a sauté pan, lightly spray with olive oil, and fry the onion, carrots, celery, and thyme over high heat for about 10 minutes, stirring regularly until softened and lightly browned, then stir in the remaining garlic and the anchovies.

Pour in the red wine, scraping the bottom of the pan with a wooden spoon to release any sediment, then add the stock, tomatoes, and tomato paste. Season with black pepper, bring to a boil, then reduce the heat and simmer for another 15–20 minutes until well reduced and thickened, stirring occasionally. Heat a grill pan, barbecue, or broiler, and cook the chops for five minutes on each side, until lightly charred and medium-rare. Season with black pepper.

Add the beans and most of the parsley to the tomato mixture and stir to combine. Season with black pepper, and cook for five minutes or until heated through. Spoon into wide-rimmed bowls, garnish with the rest of the parsley, and arrange the lamb chumps on top for serving.

PER SERVING:
606 CALORIES, 22G FAT, 7G SATURATED FAT, 44G CARBOHYDRATE, 0.9G SODIUM

lamb kofta with spiced yogurt

The Middle East uses great spices to flavor its food, and lamb absorbs them so well. The spicy meatballs and minty yogurt are an irresistible combination.

½ cup bulgur cracked wheat
2 tablespoons olive oil
1 chile, finely chopped
1 medium onion, finely chopped
½ teaspoon ground coriander
½ teaspoon ground cumin
1 pound, 2 ounces leg of lamb,
  lean, all visible fat removed, diced
1 egg
⅓ cup pine nuts, finely chopped
2 tablespoons chopped mint
2 tablespoons chopped parsley

For the the spiced yogurt
2 chiles, seeded and
  finely chopped
1 tablespoon chopped mint
1 tablespoon chopped chives,
1 tablespoon cilantro,
  finely chopped
1 tablespoon finely
  chopped parsley
1 garlic clove, crushed to a paste
½ teaspoon ground cumin
1¼ cups plain yogurt

Makes 40

Soak the bulgur in cold water for 30 minutes, drain, and squeeze dry.

Heat half the olive oil in a frying pan, then add the chile, onion, ground coriander, and cumin, and cook over low heat for 15 minutes. Drain, retaining the oil, and let cool.

Beat the egg. Place the lamb in a food processor along with the egg and the onion mix, and blend to a smooth paste. Remove, and place in a bowl along with the bulgur, pine nuts and herbs. Wet your hands and shape one teaspoon of the mixture into a small ball. Repeat to make 40 balls in total.

To make the spiced yogurt, combine all the ingredients together and leave for an hour let the flavors develop. Add the remaining oil to the reserved oil in a frying pan. Over medium heat, fry the kofta in batches, turning regularly until brown and cooked through, this should take about 10 minutes. Keep warm in the oven. Repeat until all the kofta are cooked.

Drain the kofta on absorbent paper towels and serve with the spiced yogurt dip.

PER SERVING (4 KOFTA):
188 CALORIES, 12G FAT, 4G SATURATED FAT, 8G CARBOHYDRATE, 0.08G SODIUM

shepherd's pie with a difference

Here, the cauliflower topping makes an unusual and healthier change from the traditional mashed potato. A classic English recipe.

Olive-oil spray (see page 17)
1 large onion, finely chopped
1 pound lean ground lamb
1 tablespoon all-purpose flour
2 bay leaves
1 teaspoon chopped thyme
1 teaspoon anchovy paste
$^3/_4$ cup canned chopped tomatoes
1 cup lamb, chicken, or beef stock
2 teaspoons Worcestershire sauce
Freshly ground black pepper

For the topping
1 medium cauliflower, broken into florets
2 tablespoons plain yogurt
1 egg yolk
2 tablespoons soft whole-grain bread crumbs

Serves 4

Heat a frying pan. Spray lightly with olive oil, then tip in the onion, and cook for five minutes until softened but not browned, stirring occasionally.

Meanwhile, heat a large, heavy pan and spray lightly with olive oil. Tip in half the ground lamb, and cook over a fairly high heat until evenly browned, breaking up any lumps with the back of a wooden spoon, and straining off any melted fat. Transfer to a plate. Cook the rest of the lamb, then return all of the lamb to the pan, adding the cooked onions, and stirring to combine.

Sprinkle the flour over the lamb and then add the bay leaves, thyme, and anchovy paste, stirring to combine. Add the chopped tomatoes, stock, Worcestershire sauce, and a good pinch of pepper. Bring to a boil, then reduce the heat, cover, and simmer for 45 minutes to one hour until the lamb is completely tender and softened. Season with black pepper. Let cool, then refrigerate. Remove any solidified fat from the top.

Preheat the oven to 350°F.

Meanwhile, to make the topping, place the cauliflower in a pan of boiling water, cover, and simmer for 15–20 minutes or until tender. Drain, and return to the pan for a couple of minutes to dry out, shaking the pan occasionally to prevent the cauliflower sticking to the bottom. Place the cauliflower in a food processor and blend until smooth. Place in a large bowl and beat in the yogurt and egg yolk. Season with black pepper to taste.

Spoon the lamb mixture into a two-quart casserole dish, discarding the bay leaves. Cover with the mashed cauliflower, then smooth over and mark with a spatula. Top with the bread crumbs and spray with a little oil. Bake for 25–30 minutes or until bubbling and golden brown. Serve at once straight from the dish, with a bowl of peas, if you like.

PER SERVING:
303 CALORIES, 13G FAT, 5G SATURATED FAT, 16G CARBOHYDRATE, 0.34G SODIUM

lancashire hotpot with sweet potatoes

Another traditional dish with a twist. Sweet potatoes contain more beta-carotene than ordinary potatoes. Use water instead of stock if you want to reduce the fat and sodium.

4 lamb kidneys, skinned
8 x 4-ounce lamb sirloin chops, excess fat removed
1 heaped tablespoon
  all-purpose flour
Freshly ground black pepper
1/2 tablespoon sunflower oil
2 1/2 cups fresh lamb stock
Olive-oil spray (see page 17)
1 1/2 pounds sweet potatoes, peeled
1 large floury potato, peeled
4 sprigs of thyme
2 onions, thinly sliced
2 fresh bay leaves

Serves 4

Preheat the oven to 350°F.

Place the kidneys on a cutting board and cut each one in half, then, using a small pair of scissors, remove the central core and membrane. Place in a bowl along with the lamb chops, add the flour, and season generously with black pepper. Toss to coat, shaking off any excess.

Heat a large non-stick frying pan. Add the oil and brown the chops for two to three minutes on each side – you may have to do this in batches depending on the size of the pan. Transfer to a plate and set aside. Add the kidneys to the frying pan and fry for one to two minutes on each side, then add to the plate with the chops. Tip away any excess fat from the pan, then add a little of the stock to deglaze, scraping the bottom with a wooden spoon to remove any sediment.

Spray a heavy five-quart casserole dish with a little oil. Cut the sweet potatoes into half-inch slices. Thinly slice the floury potato and set aside for the top of the hotpot. Line the bottom of the dish with half of the sweet potato slices. Place four of the chops on top, then add two thyme sprigs and half of the onions. Season with black pepper to taste and pop the kidneys around the sides of the casserole dish. Repeat the layers with the remaining ingredients and then pour in the stock that was used to deglaze the pan, along with the remaining stock.

Finally, arrange an overlapping layer of the floury potato on top. Spray a little olive oil over the potato, cover, and bake in the oven for two and a half hours until the lamb is completely tender, removing the lid for the final 30 minutes to let the potatoes go golden brown.

Serve the Lancashire hotpot straight from the casserole dish, with bowls of steamed broccoli and carrots.

PER SERVING:
569 CALORIES, 18G FAT, 8G SATURATED FAT, 53G CARBOHYDRATE, 0.5G SODIUM

desserts

peach and blueberry gratin

So simple, so delicious, this gratin should evoke gasps of delight and anticipation from your guests. This is an elegant dessert that won't cause you too much stress to make.

4 canned peach halves in natural juice
1/2 cup blueberries
2 ounces mascarpone cheese (about 1/4 cup)
3/4 cup plain yogurt
1 tablespoon sugar
1/2 teaspoon ground cinnamon

Serves 4

Place the peach halves in the bottom of four ramekin dishes and top with the blueberries.

Beat together the mascarpone and yogurt with a wooden spoon, then pour it over the fruit. Combine the sugar and cinnamon, then sprinkle it over the yogurt mix.

Preheat the broiler to its highest setting. Place the ramekins under the broiler for five to six minutes until the sugar is golden. Alternatively, glaze using a cook's blow torch, chef-style. Let cool for a couple of minutes, and serve.

PER SERVING:
133 CALORIES, 8G FAT, 5G SATURATED FAT, 12G CARBOHYDRATE, 0.05G SODIUM

raspberry-ripple zabaglione

A wonderfully light and moussy custard, adorned with fresh raspberries. The slightly sharp taste of the fruit adds a little zing to this dessert.

1 1/2 cups raspberries
Juice of 1/2 lemon
2 teaspoons confectioners' sugar
4 egg yolks
1 tablespoon superfine sugar
2 tablespoons medium-dry sherry
2 tablespoons dry white wine
1/4 cup plain yogurt

Serves 4

Reserve 12 raspberries for decoration and place the rest in a food processor along with a good squeeze of lemon juice. Blitz to a purée, then push the fruit through a wire mesh strainer to remove the seeds. Add confectioners' sugar to taste, leaving the fruit slightly on the tart side, then set aside.

Place the egg yolks and superfine sugar in a large, heatproof bowl. Beat in the sherry and wine, using a whisk. Place over a pan of simmering water and heat gently, whisking continuously until the mixture is very light but holds its shape. Alternatively, you may use a double boiler. When it is the consistency of semi-melted ice cream, remove from the heat and continue to whisk, this time over a bowl of iced water, until cool – this prevents it from splitting.

Fold the yogurt into the mixture. Drizzle in the raspberry purée and gently swirl to create a ripple effect. Spoon into stemmed serving glasses, decorate with the reserved raspberries, and serve with wafer-thin biscuits, if you like.

PER SERVING:
126 CALORIES, 6G FAT, 2G SATURATED FAT, 10G CARBOHYDRATE, 0.02G SODIUM

mango fool with mango sauce

Mango and lime is a truly wonderful marriage of flavors. This refreshing dessert is especially welcome after a heavy meal.

2 egg yolks
2 tablespoons superfine sugar
2 tablespoons Kirsch (optional)
Juice of 2 limes
$3/4$ cup plain yogurt
2 mangoes, peeled, pitted and puréed

Serves 4

Place a bowl over a saucepan of simmering water, add the egg yolks and sugar, and beat until the mixture has thickened and trebled in volume, this should take about 10 minutes. Alternatively, you may use a double boiler to do this. Remove the bowl and sit it over ice. Whisk until cold, then place in the refrigerator.

Once its chilled, add half the Kirsch (if using) and half the lime juice to the egg mixture. In a separate bowl, whip the yogurt lightly and fold into two-thirds of the mango purée. Then fold this into the egg mixture. Pour into glasses or bowls, and refrigerate.

Whisk the remaining Kirsch (if using), lime juice, and mango purée together and pour it over the mango fool for serving.

PER SERVING:
177 CALORIES, 5G FAT, 2G SATURATED FAT, 29G CARBOHYDRATE, 0.04G SODIUM

poached figs with raspberries in red wine

Figs have found more favor in savory food, but this dish will return them to their rightful place among desserts.

1 pound ripe raspberries or blackberries
Juice of 2 lemons
Juice of 1 orange
$1/4$ cup superfine sugar
1 glass Zinfandel red wine
8 firm fresh figs
3 tablespoons crème de mure (blackberry liqueur) or crème de cassis (black currant liqueur) – optional
1 tablespoon freshly chopped mint
Low-fat fromage frais or yogurt, for serving

Serves 4

Place the berries in a food processor along with the lemon and orange juice, and blend until smooth. Strain the purée through a fine mesh strainer into a non-reactive (not aluminum) saucepan. Discard the seeds.

Add the sugar and the red wine to the berry purée and place the pan over medium heat. Bring to a boil and simmer gently, skimming off any scum that might rise to the surface. When the sugar has dissolved, add the figs, and poach for five to six minutes depending on their ripeness. Remove the figs to a glass bowl when cooked.

Reduce the berry cooking liquor to approximately one and a quarter cups. Let cool. Add the crème de mure or cassis, if using, and mint, and pour them over the figs. Cover and chill overnight. Serve with low-fat fromage frais, or, if unavailable, low-fat yogurt.

PER SERVING:
153 CALORIES, 0.6G FAT, 0G SATURATED FAT, 31G CARBOHYDRATE, 0.01G SODIUM

nutty apple tart with a twist

The combination of sweet Granny Smith and tart cooking apples works well here, while the cinnamon and cloves add a touch of the exotic to a classic dish.

4 Granny Smith apples, peeled, cut in half, and cored
Juice of 1 lemon
2 tart cooking apples, peeled, cored, and diced
$1/4$ cup superfine sugar
$1/2$ teaspoon ground cinnamon
$1/2$ teaspoon ground cloves
Prepared pie dough, enough for a 9-inch pie
$1/4$ cup hazelnuts, toasted and chopped
1 egg, beaten
1 tablespoon confectioners' sugar

Serves 6

Place the Granny Smith apples in a bowl along with the lemon juice and pour in enough water to cover. Place the cooking apples in a saucepan along with three tablespoons water, cover, and simmer for 20 minutes, stirring occasionally. Remove the lid and beat in the superfine sugar, cinnamon, and cloves until you have a smooth purée. Remove from the heat and let cool completely. Roll the dough on a lightly floured counter to a 9-inch square, then trim the edges. Transfer to a baking sheet lined with wax paper and chill for at least 30 minutes. Drain the Granny Smith apples and slice each half into eight thin slices.

Preheat the oven to 400°F. Remove the dough from the fridge and spread the purée over the dough, leaving a half-inch border around the edges. Sprinkle the hazelnuts on the dough, then top with the apple slices in overlapping layers. Brush the exposed border of the dough with the beaten egg. Bake for 15–20 minutes or until the edges are puffed up and golden brown, and the apple slices are tender and lightly golden.

Remove the tart from the oven and sprinkle enough confectioners' sugar over it to cover the apple slices. Using a cook's blow torch, caramelize the apples; alternatively place the tart under a very hot broiler for a few seconds. Cut the tart into slices and serve with a little vanilla custard (page 135), if you like.

PER SERVING:
308 CALORIES, 14G FAT, 6G SATURATED FAT, 43G CARBOHYDRATE, 0.08G SODIUM

pineapple carpaccio with a fruit "daiquiri" sauce

Thin slices of pineapple in a fruity cocktail. This dessert is as low in fat as it is high in flavor

1 medium pineapple, peeled, cored, and "eyes" removed
2 ripe bananas, peeled
1 cup ripe strawberries, hulled
3 tablespoons plain yogurt
2 tablespoons dark rum
1 tablespoon honey
4 sprigs of mint

Serves 4

Using a sharp knife, cut the pineapple into paper-thin slices and arrange them so they cover the bottom of four large plates.

In a blender, puree together the bananas, strawberries (reserving four for decoration), yogurt, rum, and honey until smooth.

Slice the four reserved strawberries. Drizzle the fruit sauce over the pineapple and decorate with the strawberries and mint sprigs.

PER SERVING:
157 CALORIES, 1G FAT, 1G SATURATED FAT, 32G CARBOHYDRATE, 0.02G SODIUM

fruit salad with kiwi juices

Here's a fruit salad with a twist – the sweet, slightly spicy wine complements the fruits admirably. Something for the summer: light, fruity, and no leftovers!

1¼ cups Gerwurztraminer wine
2 tablespoons honey
6 kiwi fruit, peeled
2 Granny Smith apples, peeled and cored
2 tablespoons lemon juice
1 mango, peeled, pitted and diced
10 large strawberries, hulled and cut in half
½ pineapple, peeled, cored, "eyes" removed, and cubed

Serves 4

Bring the wine and honey to a boil and then let cool to room temperature.

In a food processor, blend four of the kiwi fruit with the wine and honey mix. If you don't like the seeds of kiwi fruit, push them through a fine mesh strainer. Cut each of the remaining kiwi into eight wedges.

Dice the apples and toss with the lemon juice. Combine with the other fruits.

Arrange the fruit salad in the center of your bowl, ladle the kiwi juice around them, and chill until ready to eat. Serve with the kiwi wedges.

PER SERVING:
253 CALORIES, 1G FAT, 0G SATURATED FAT, 50G CARBOHYDRATE, 0.02G SODIUM

fruity apple crisp

Miss your cobbler? This is the next best thing. Full of fruit and spice and all things nice, the muesli or granola makes a wonderfully crispy, yet healthy topping.

3 Granny Smith apples, peeled, cored, and each cut into 8
2 peaches, peeled, pitted, and each cut into 6
$^1/_4$ cup mixed dried fruits (cranberries, blueberries, cherries)
1 tablespoon soft dark brown sugar
$^1/_2$ teaspoon ground cinnamon
$^1/_2$ teaspoon apple spice
Juice and grated peel of 1 orange
2 tablespoons all-purpose flour
$1^1/_2$ cups unsweetened muesli or granola

Serves 6

Preheat the oven to 350°F.

Combine all the ingredients, except the muesli or granola, and spoon into a baking dish. Sprinkle with the muesli or granola and bake in the oven for about 45 minutes, until golden and the fruit is bubbling. Serve with Vanilla Custard (see right).

PER SERVING:
203 CALORIES, 3G FAT, 0.4G SATURATED FAT, 43G CARBOHYDRATE, 0.02G SODIUM

vanilla custard

A classic custard, this is the healthy version that you will turn to again and again. The vanilla beans give it a seductive fragrance. Serve with your favorite fruity puddings.

2 tablespoons cornstarch
4 teaspoons superfine sugar
$2^1/_2$ cups skim milk
1 vanilla bean or 1 teaspoon vanilla extract
2 egg yolks

Serves 4

Mix the cornstarch and sugar with a little milk to form a paste, then add the remaining milk.

Split the vanilla bean lengthwise and, with the tip of a small knife, scrape the seeds into the milk, then pop the bean into the milk as well, or add the vanilla extract instead.

Cook the milk over low heat until the mixture boils and thickens. Remove the vanilla bean, if using, and slowly whisk the milk into the egg yolks. Return to the heat and cook very slowly, stirring continuously until the custard coats the back of the spoon. Do not let it boil. Serve hot or cold.

PER SERVING:
129 CALORIES, 3G FAT, 1G SATURATED FAT, 20G CARBOHYDRATE, 0.09G SODIUM

fruity rice pudding

This pudding has nothing in common with the rice puddings you might have eaten in the past.
The real deal, full of flavor and fruit, and made with brown rice for extra fiber.

½ cup brown rice, washed
1¹/₂ cups skim milk
4 medium eggs
2 tablespoons margarine, softened
¹/₃ cup superfine sugar
¹/₃ cup mixed dried fruits (cranberries, cherries, blueberries, golden raisins)
¹/₂ teaspoon ground cinnamon
1 cup raspberries

Serves 6

Bring the rice and milk to a boil in a saucepan, then reduce the heat and cook, covered, until most of the milk has evaporated into the rice, this should take about one and a half hours.

Preheat the oven to 350°F.

In a bowl, beat the eggs. Fold the eggs into the rice, a little at a time, then add the margarine and the sugar.

Dust the dried fruits with cinnamon, then add them to the rice mixture.

Put a few raspberries in the bottom of six ramekins, then spoon the rice over the raspberries. Place the ramekins in a roasting tray and pour warm water into the tray until it reaches halfway up the sides of the ramekins. Bake in the oven for 50 minutes, and eat hot or cold.

PER SERVING:
248 CALORIES, 8G FAT, 2G SATURATED FAT, 39G CARBOHYDRATE, 0.11G SODIUM

chocolate steamed pudding

Everybody loves chocolate, and this is perfect for the occasional treat. Good-quality chocolate tends to be lower in saturated fat than normal chocolate.

2 squares (2 ounces) unsweetened baking chocolate
   (ideally minimum 70 percent cocoa solids)
1 cup all-purpose flour
¹/₂ cup sugar
1 tablespoon unsweetened cocoa powder
¹/₂ cup skim milk
1 egg
1 teaspoon baking powder
¹/₂ teaspoon grated nutmeg
³/₄ cup hazelnuts, toasted and chopped
Margarine, for greasing

Serves 6

Melt the chocolate in a bowl set over a saucepan of simmering water. Alternatively, use a double boiler.

Combine the remaining ingredients, except for the hazelnuts, in a food processor or mixer and blend for one minute at low speed. Add the melted chocolate and blend for one minute at high speed. Fold in the hazelnuts.

Lightly grease a two-and-a-half-cup pudding bowl with margarine. Spoon the batter into the bowl. Cover with a lid, or else cover with a pleated greased sheet of foil and tie securely with string. Set a rack in the bottom of a saucepan, and place the pudding bowl on the rack. Pour boiling water into the saucepan until it comes three-quarters of the way up the side of the bowl. Cook over medium heat for about one and a half hours or until a knife or skewer inserted into the center of the pudding comes out clean.

Remove the pudding bowl from the saucepan and let cool for 10 minutes. Run a knife around the edge to loosen, and invert onto a serving dish. Serve with Vanilla Custard (see page 135).

PER SERVING:
289 CALORIES, 13G FAT, 3G SATURATED FAT, 39G CARBOHYDRATE, 0.14G SODIUM

bread and butter pudding
with raspberry sauce

Comfort food that we all need from time to time, this is a much-loved recipe that is worth the effort.

$^1/_4$ cup golden raisins
$^1/_4$ cup raisins
$^1/_4$ cup strong tea
1 tablespoon brandy extract or flavoring
14 slices medium-cut whole-grain bread
$^1/_3$ cup unsalted margarine, softened
4 eggs, plus 2 egg yolks
$^1/_2$ cup confectioners' sugar
2 teaspoons vanilla extract
3 cups skim milk
Pinch of grated nutmeg
2 tablespoons superfine sugar

For the raspberry sauce
1 cup fresh raspberries
1 teaspoon confectioners' sugar
Juice of 2 limes

Serves 8

Place the raisins in a small non-metallic bowl and pour the tea and the brandy extract over them. Cover with plastic wrap and let soak for at least two hours (overnight is best). Drain off any excess juices and reserve.

Spread the bread with the margarine. Remove the crusts and cut each slice into four triangles. Grease a two-and-a-half-quart shallow ovenproof dish with a little of the remaining margarine and arrange a layer of the bread triangles in the bottom of the dish, margarine-side up. Scatter half of the soaked dried fruits over them, and place another layer of the bread triangles on top, margarine-side up – you should have used about two-thirds of them at this stage. Set the remainder

aside. Scatter over the remaining soaked dried fruits and press down gently into the dish with a spatula.

Whisk together the eggs, egg yolks, and the confectioners' sugar in a large pitcher. Add the vanilla extract and milk, whisking to combine. Pour two-thirds of this custard over the layered bread triangles and let stand for 45 minutes to an hour until the bread has soaked up all of the custard.

Preheat the oven to 350°F.

Pour the remaining custard mixture over the soaked bread and margarine triangles. Arrange the rest of the bread triangles on top, margarine-side up. Press the slices down firmly with a spatula so that the custard comes halfway up the bread triangles. Sprinkle the nutmeg and superfine sugar on top.

Place the dish into a roasting pan and pour warm water into the roasting pan so that it comes three-quarters of the way up the dish. Bake for 35–40 minutes or until the custard has just set and the top is golden brown.

To make the sauce, place all the ingredients in a blender and puree until smooth. Push through a fine mesh strainer to remove the seeds. Refrigerate until ready to serve.

Drizzle some raspberry sauce over the pudding and serve.

PER SERVING:
361 CALORIES, 14G FAT, 4G SATURATED FAT, 49G CARBOHYDRATE, 0.47G SODIUM

index

resources

US

Diabetes Wellness and Research Foundation
1206 Potomac Street
Washington D.C. 20007
D.C. office: 1-877-633-3976
Helpline 1-800-941-4635
www.diabeteswellness.net

American Diabetes Association
ATTN: National Call Center
1701 North Beauregard street
Alexandria, VA 22311
1-800-DIABETES (342-2383)
www.diabetes.org

Diabetes Exercise and Sports Foundation (DESA)
8001 Montcastle Drive
Nashville
TN 37221
1-800-898-4322
www.diabetes-exercise.org

Juvenile Diabetes Research Foundation International
120 Wall Street
New York
NY 10005-4001
1-800-533-CURE (2873)
www.jdrf.org

CANADA

Canadian Diabetes Association
National:
1-800-BANTING (226-8464)
Local: 1-416-363-3373
www.diabetes.ca

CANADA

Juvenile Diabetes Research Foundation
Head Office, 7100 Woodbine Avenue, Suite 311, Markham, Ontario L3R 5J2
1-905-944-8700
Toll-free 1-877-CURE-533
www.jdrf.ca

UK

Diabetes Research & Wellness Foundation
Office 101/102, Northney Marina
Hayling Island, Hampshire PO11 0NH
011 44 (0)23 9263 7808
(Admin and Enquiries)
011 44 (0)23 9263 6132 (Publications)
www.diabeteswellnessnet.org.uk

www.thinkwelltobewell.com
azmina.govindji@virgin.net

AUSTRALIA

Diabetes Australia
G.P.O. Box 3156, Canberra ACT 2601
Freecall helpline: 1300 136 588
www.diabetesaustralia.com.au

Acknowledgments

Writing this book has been a great pleasure for me. This was made almost effortless by the co-operation of Antony, who tirelessly took on the sometimes challenging requests. I also have been supported by Muna Reyal, who has been understanding and obliging throughout. Special people have shaped my writing – the inspirational life coach Nina Puddefoot, dietitian and lecturer Sue Baic, my husband, Shamil, and my children, Shazia and Bizhan. Lastly, I would like to acknowledge the trust which the Diabetes Research and Wellness Foundation has placed in me. AG

There are too many people to thank, but certain individuals deserve a special mention:
To my wonderful wife, Jacinta, and our two children, Toby and Billie, who suffered from my lack of quality time yet supported me throughout as I managed to juggle my time through three books, and everything else going on in my life.
To Louise, my energetic and ultra-efficient personal assistant, who fielded hundreds of phone calls from the publishers and who was regularly on hand to smooth troubled waters when the pressures of deadlines occasionally took their toll.
To Fiona Lindsay, Linda Shanks, and Lesley Turnbull at Limelight Management, who are constantly there to make sure I have more than enough work to handle.
To my team at Notting Grill, especially David, George, and Candido, who kept the boat afloat in my often extended absences.
To the various friends Nicki, Kate, Sarah, Margot, Suzie, June, Anne and John, and Mike and Nicky, who acted unknowingly as guinea pigs for many of the recipes.
To Azmina Govindji, who waited patiently for the recipes so that she could nutritionally analyze them, and for producing an excellent section on the whys and wherefores of diabetes, much of which I had limited knowledge of.
And finally to Muna Reyal, my editor, and her fab team at Kyle Cathie for giving me the opportunity to produce this cookbook. They turned my offerings into a beautifully executed book that people with diabetes will find easy to understand, and hopefully they will realize life doesn't have to change that much when it comes to eating. AWT